1A

W9-CCC-776

Grammar in Context

4TH EDITION

SANDRA N. ELBAUM

THOMSON

HEINLE

Australia • Canada • Mexico • Singapore • Spain • United Kingdom • United States

THOMSON

―✴―™

HEINLE

Grammar in Context 1A, Fourth Edition
ELBAUM

Publisher, Adult & Academic: *James W. Brown*
Senior Acquisitions Editor, Adult & Academic:
  Sherrise Roehr
Director of Product Development: *Anita Raducanu*
Associate Development Editor: *Yeny Kim*
Production Manager: *Sally Giangrande*
Director of Marketing: *Amy Mabley*
Marketing Manager: *Laura Needham*
Senior Print Buyer: *Mary Beth Hennebury*

Development Editor: *Charlotte Sturdy*
Compositor: *Nesbitt Graphics, Inc.*
Project Manager: *Lois Lombardo*
Photo Researcher: *Connie Gardner*
Illustrators: *Ralph Canaday, James Edwards,*
  Larry Frederick, and Brock Nichol
Interior Designer: *Jerilyn Bockorick*
Cover Designer: *Joseph Sherman*
Printer: *Edwards Brothers*

Cover Image: Brooklyn Bridge, New York by Julian Barrow/Private Collection/Bridgeman Art Library

For permission to use material from this text or product, submit a request online at http://www.thomsonrights.com

Any additional questions about permissions can be submitted by email to thomsonrights@thomson.com

ISBN: 1-4130-0737-6

Printed in the United States of America.
1 2 3 4 5 6 7 8 9 10   09 08 07 06 05

For more information contact Thomson Heinle, 25 Thomson Place, Boston, Massachusetts 02210 USA, or you can visit our Internet site at elt.thomson.com

Photo credits appear on page C1, which constitutes a continuation of this copyright page.

Contents

Lesson 3   77

Lesson 4   101

Lesson 5   131

Lesson 6   159

Lesson 7   189

Lesson 8   223

Lesson 9   263

Lesson 13   377

GRAMMAR Auxiliary Verbs with *Too* and *Either*; Auxiliary Verbs in Tag Questions

CONTEXT Dating and Marriage

Lesson 14   401

GRAMMAR Verb Review

CONTEXT Washington Interns

Appendices

In memory of

Herman and Ethel Elbaum

Acknowledgments

Many thanks to Dennis Hogan, Jim Brown, Sherrise Roehr, Yeny Kim, and Sally Giangrande from Thomson Heinle for their ongoing support of the *Grammar in Context* series. I would especially like to thank my editor, Charlotte Sturdy, for her keen eye to detail and invaluable suggestions.

And many thanks to my students at Truman College, who have increased my understanding of my own language and taught me to see life from another point of view. By sharing their observations, questions, and life stories, they have enriched my life enormously—*Sandra N. Elbaum*

Heinle would like to thank the following people for their contributions:

Marki Alexander
Oklahoma State
 University
Stillwater, OK

Joan M. Amore
Triton College
River Grove, IL

Edina Pingleton Bagley
Nassau Community
 College
Garden City, NY

Judith A. G. Benka
Normandale Community
 College
Bloomington, MN

Judith Book-Ehrlichman
Bergen Community
 College
Paramus, NJ

Lyn Buchheit
Community College of
 Philadelphia
Philadelphia, PA

Charlotte M. Calobrisi
Northern Virginia
 Community College
Annandale, VA

Sarah A. Carpenter
Normandale Community
 College
Bloomington, MN

Jeanette Clement
Duquesne University
Pittsburgh, PA

Allis Cole
Shoreline Community
 College
Shoreline, WA

Jacqueline M. Cunningham
Triton College
River Grove, IL

Lisa DePaoli
Sierra College
Rocklin, CA

Maha Edlbi
Sierra College
Rocklin, CA

Rhonda J. Farley
Cosumnes River College
Sacramento, CA

Jennifer Farnell
University of Connecticut
American Language
 Program
Stamford, CT

Abigail-Marie Fiattarone
Mesa Community College
Mesa, AZ

Marcia Gethin-Jones
University of Connecticut
American Language
 Program
Storrs, CT

Linda Harlow
Santa Rosa Junior
 College
Santa Rosa, CA

Suha R. Hattab
Triton College
River Grove, IL

Bill Keniston
Normandale Community
 College
Bloomington, MN

Walton King
Arkansas State
 University
Jonesboro, AR

Kathleen Krokar
Truman College
Chicago, IL

John Larkin
NVCC-Community and
 Workforce
 Development
Annandale, VA

Michael Larsen
American River College
Sacramento, CA

Bea C. Lawn
Gavilan College
Gilroy, CA

Rob Lee
Pasadena City College
Pasadena, CA

Oranit Limmaneeprasert
American River College
Sacramento, CA

Gennell Lockwood
Shoreline Community
 College
Shoreline, WA

Linda Louie
Highline Community
 College
Des Moines, WA

Melanie A. Majeski
Naugatuck Valley
 Community College
Waterbury, CT

Maria Marin
De Anza College
Cupertino, CA

Karen Miceli
Cosumnes River College
Sacramento, CA

Jeanie Pavichevich
Triton College
River Grove, IL

Herbert Pierson
St. John's University
New York City, NY

Dina Poggi
De Anza College
Cupertino, CA

Mark Rau
American River College
Sacramento, CA

John W. Roberts
Shoreline Community
 College
Shoreline, WA

Azize R. Ruttler
Bergen Community
 College
Paramus, NJ

Ann Salzmann
University of Illinois,
Urbana, IL

Eva Teagarden
Yuba College
Marysville, CA

Susan Wilson
San Jose City College
San Jose, CA

Martha Yeager-Tobar
Cerritos College
Norwalk, CA

A word from the author

It seems that I was born to be an ESL teacher. My parents immigrated to the U.S. from Poland as adults and were confused not only by the English language but by American culture as well. Born in the U.S., I often had the task as a child to explain the intricacies of the language and allay my parents' fears about the culture. It is no wonder to me that I became an ESL teacher, and later, an ESL writer who focuses on explanations of American culture in order to illustrate grammar. My life growing up in an immigrant neighborhood was very similar to the lives of my students, so I have a feel for what confuses them and what they need to know about American life.

ESL teachers often find themselves explaining confusing customs and providing practical information about life in the U.S. Often, teachers are a student's only source of information about American life. With **Grammar in Context, Fourth Edition,** I enjoy sharing my experiences with you.

Grammar in Context, Fourth Edition connects grammar with American cultural context, providing learners of English with a useful and meaningful skill and knowledge base. Students learn the grammar necessary to communicate verbally and in writing, and learn how American culture plays a role in language, beliefs, and everyday situations.

Enjoy the new edition of **Grammar in Context!**

Sandra N. Elbaum

Grammar in Context

Students learn more, remember more, and use language more effectively when they learn grammar in context.

Learning a language through meaningful themes and practicing it in a contextualized setting promote both linguistic and cognitive development. In **Grammar in Context**, grammar is presented in interesting and culturally informative readings, and the language and context are subsequently practiced throughout the chapter.

New to this edition:

- **New and updated readings** on current American topics such as Instant Messaging and eBay.
- **Updated grammar charts** that now include essential language notes.
- **Updated exercises and activities** that provide contextualized practice using a variety of exercise types, as well as additional practice for more difficult structures.
- **New lower-level *Grammar in Context Basic*** for beginning level students.
- **New wrap-around Teacher's Annotated Edition** with page-by-page, point-of-use teaching suggestions.
- **Expanded Assessment CD-ROM** with ExamView ® Pro Test Generator now contains more questions types and assessment options to easily allow teachers to create tests and quizzes.

Distinctive Features of *Grammar in Context:*

Students are prepared for academic assignments and everyday language tasks.

Discussions, readings, compositions, and exercises involving higher-level critical thinking skills develop overall language and communication skills.

Students expand their knowledge of American topics and culture.

The readings in **Grammar in Context** help students gain insight into and enrich their knowledge of American culture and history. Students gain ample exposure to the practicalities of American life, such as writing a résumé, dealing with telemarketers, and junk mail, and getting student internships. Their new knowledge helps them adapt to everyday life in the U.S.

Students learn to use their new skills to communicate.

The exercises and Expansion Activities in **Grammar in Context** help students learn English while practicing their writing and speaking skills. Students work together in pairs and groups to find more information about topics, to make presentations, to play games, and to role-play. Their confidence in using English increases, as does their ability to communicate effectively.

Welcome to **Grammar in Context, Fourth Edition**

Students learn more, remember more, and use language more effectively when they learn grammar in context.

Grammar in Context, Fourth Edition connects grammar with rich, American cultural context, providing learners of English with a useful and meaningful skill and knowledge base.

An **Audio Program** allows students to hear the readings and dialogs, and provides an opportunity to practice their listening skills.

Readings on American topics such as Instant Messaging, eBay, and The AIDS Ride present and illustrate the grammatical structure in an informative and meaningful context.

Grammar charts offer clear explanations and provide contextualized examples of the structure.

Language Notes refine students' understanding of the target structure.

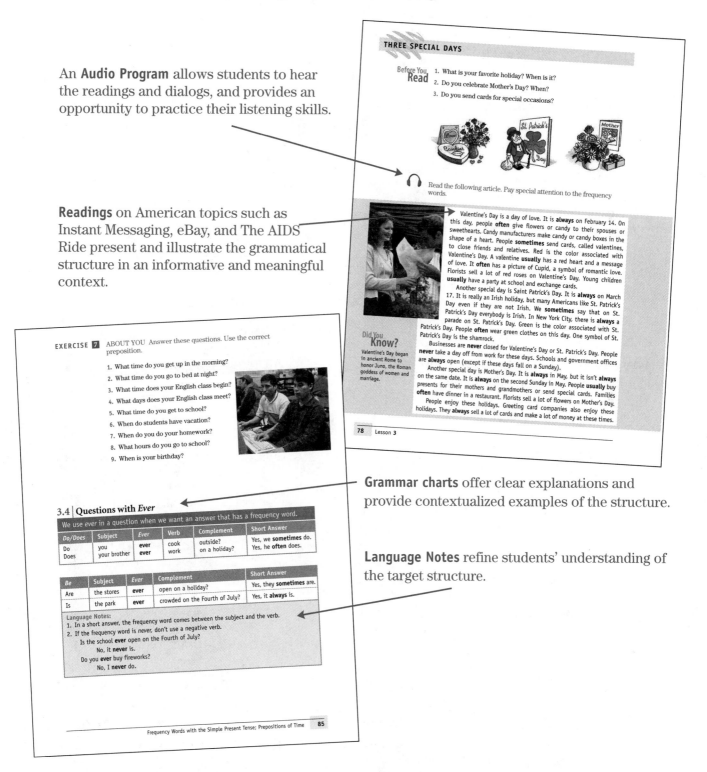

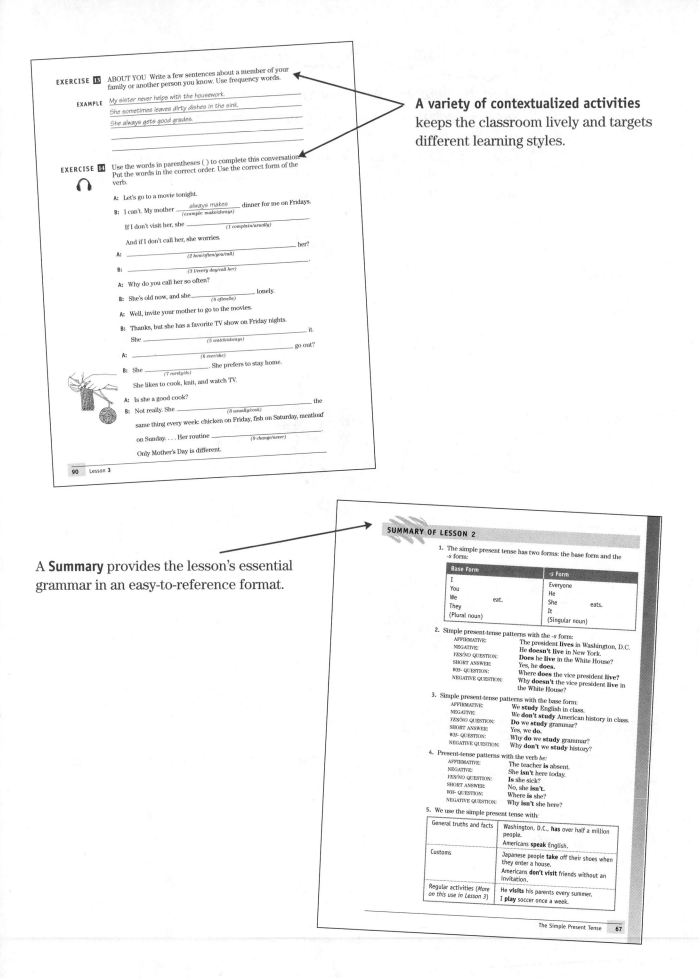

EXERCISE 13 ABOUT YOU Write a few sentences about a member of your family or another person you know. Use frequency words.

EXAMPLE My sister never helps with the housework.
She sometimes leaves dirty dishes in the sink.
She always gets good grades.

_____
_____
_____

EXERCISE 14 Use the words in parentheses ( ) to complete this conversation. Put the words in the correct order. Use the correct form of the verb.

A: Let's go to a movie tonight.

B: I can't. My mother ___always makes___ dinner for me on Fridays.
                    (example: make/always)

If I don't visit her, she _____.
                          (1 complain/usually)

And if I don't call her, she worries.

A: _____ her?
        (2 how/often/you/call)

B: _____.
        (3 I/every day/call her)

A: Why do you call her so often?

B: She's old now, and she _____ lonely.
                            (4 often/be)

A: Well, invite your mother to go to the movies.

B: Thanks, but she has a favorite TV show on Friday nights.
She _____ it.
        (5 watch/always)

A: _____ go out?
        (6 ever/she)

B: She _____. She prefers to stay home.
        (7 rarely/do)

She likes to cook, knit, and watch TV.

A: Is she a good cook?

B: Not really. She _____ the
                    (8 usually/cook)

same thing every week: chicken on Friday, fish on Saturday, meatloaf

on Sunday. . . . Her routine _____.
                              (9 change/never)

Only Mother's Day is different.

A variety of contextualized activities keeps the classroom lively and targets different learning styles.

A **Summary** provides the lesson's essential grammar in an easy-to-reference format.

SUMMARY OF LESSON 2

1. The simple present tense has two forms: the base form and the -s form:

Base Form		-s Form	
I		Everyone	
You		He	
We	eat.	She	eats.
They		It	
(Plural noun)		(Singular noun)	

2. Simple present-tense patterns with the -s form:

AFFIRMATIVE:	The president **lives** in Washington, D.C.
NEGATIVE:	He **doesn't live** in New York.
YES/NO QUESTION:	**Does** he **live** in the White House?
SHORT ANSWER:	Yes, he **does.**
WH- QUESTION:	Where **does** the vice president **live?**
NEGATIVE QUESTION:	Why **doesn't** the vice president **live** in the White House?

3. Simple present-tense patterns with the base form:

AFFIRMATIVE:	We **study** English in class.
NEGATIVE:	We **don't study** American history in class.
YES/NO QUESTION:	**Do** we **study** grammar?
SHORT ANSWER:	Yes, we **do.**
WH- QUESTION:	Why **do** we **study** grammar?
NEGATIVE QUESTION:	Why **don't** we **study** history?

4. Present-tense patterns with the verb be:

AFFIRMATIVE:	The teacher **is** absent.
NEGATIVE:	She **isn't** here today.
YES/NO QUESTION:	**Is** she sick?
SHORT ANSWER:	No, she **isn't.**
WH- QUESTION:	Where **is** she?
NEGATIVE QUESTION:	Why **isn't** she here?

5. We use the simple present tense with:

General truths and facts	Washington, D.C., **has** over half a million people.
	Americans **speak** English.
Customs	Japanese people **take** off their shoes when they enter a house.
	Americans **don't visit** friends without an invitation.
Regular activities (More on this use in Lesson 3)	He **visits** his parents every summer.
	I **play** soccer once a week.

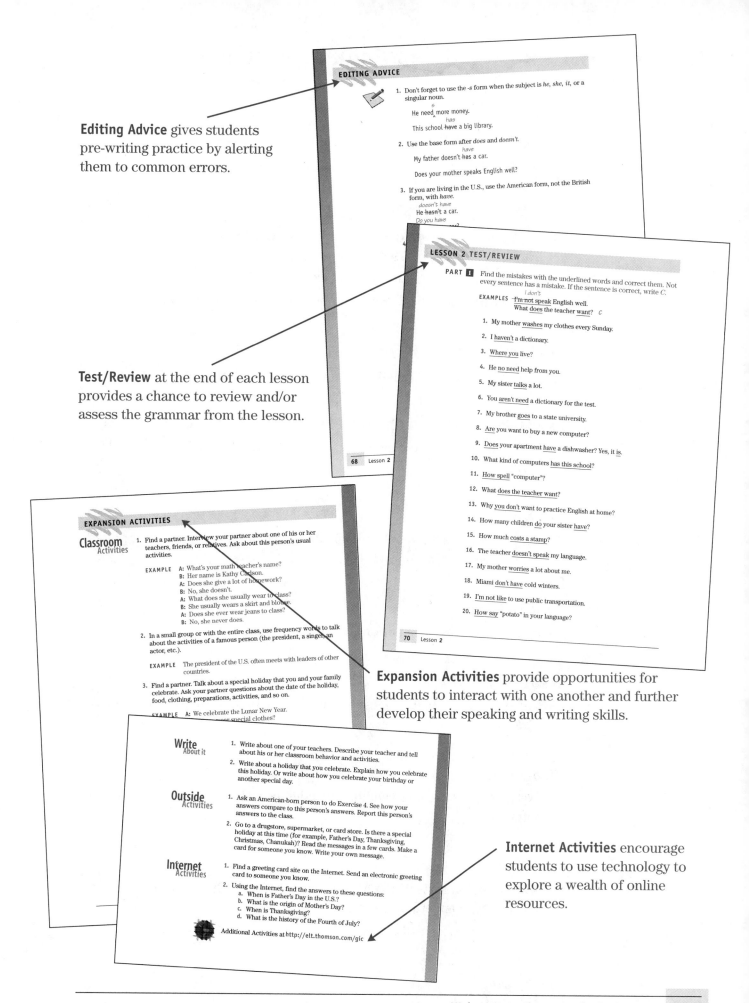

Editing Advice gives students pre-writing practice by alerting them to common errors.

EDITING ADVICE

1. Don't forget to use the *-s* form when the subject is *he, she, it,* or a singular noun.

   He need more money.

   This school have a big library.

2. Use the base form after *does* and *doesn't.*

   My father doesn't has a car.

   Does your mother speaks English well?

3. If you are living in the U.S., use the American form, not the British form, with *have.*

   He hasn't a car.

   Do you have

Test/Review at the end of each lesson provides a chance to review and/or assess the grammar from the lesson.

LESSON 2 TEST/REVIEW

PART I Find the mistakes with the underlined words and correct them. Not every sentence has a mistake. If the sentence is correct, write *C.*

EXAMPLES I'm not speak English well.

What does the teacher want? *C*

1. My mother washes my clothes every Sunday.
2. I haven't a dictionary.
3. Where you live?
4. He no need help from you.
5. My sister talks a lot.
6. You aren't need a dictionary for the test.
7. My brother goes to a state university.
8. Are you want to buy a new computer?
9. Does your apartment have a dishwasher? Yes, it is.
10. What kind of computers has this school?
11. How spell "computer"?
12. What does the teacher want?
13. Why you don't want to practice English at home?
14. How many children do your sister have?
15. How much costs a stamp?
16. The teacher doesn't speak my language.
17. My mother worries a lot about me.
18. Miami don't have cold winters.
19. I'm not like to use public transportation.
20. How say "potato" in your language?

70 Lesson 2

68 Lesson 2

EXPANSION ACTIVITIES

Classroom Activities

1. Find a partner. Interview your partner about one of his or her teachers, friends, or relatives. Ask about this person's usual activities.

   EXAMPLE A: What's your math teacher's name?
   B: Her name is Kathy Carlson.
   A: Does she give a lot of homework?
   B: No, she doesn't.
   A: What does she usually wear to class?
   B: She usually wears a skirt and blouse.
   A: Does she ever wear jeans to class?
   B: No, she never does.

2. In a small group or with the entire class, use frequency words to talk about the activities of a famous person (the president, a singer, an actor, etc.).

   EXAMPLE The president of the U.S. often meets with leaders of other countries.

3. Find a partner. Talk about a special holiday that you and your family celebrate. Ask your partner questions about the date of the holiday, food, clothing, preparations, activities, and so on.

   EXAMPLE A: We celebrate the Lunar New Year.

Expansion Activities provide opportunities for students to interact with one another and further develop their speaking and writing skills.

Write About it

1. Write about one of your teachers. Describe your teacher and tell about his or her classroom behavior and activities.

2. Write about a holiday that you celebrate. Explain how you celebrate this holiday. Or write about how you celebrate your birthday or another special day.

Outside Activities

1. Ask an American-born person to do Exercise 4. See how your answers compare to this person's answers. Report this person's answers to the class.

2. Go to a drugstore, supermarket, or card store. Is there a special holiday at this time (for example, Father's Day, Thanksgiving, Christmas, Chanukah)? Read the messages in a few cards. Make a card for someone you know. Write your own message.

Internet Activities

1. Find a greeting card site on the Internet. Send an electronic greeting card to someone you know.

2. Using the Internet, find the answers to these questions:
   a. When is Father's Day in the U.S.?
   b. What is the origin of Mother's Day?
   c. When is Thanksgiving?
   d. What is the history of the Fourth of July?

Additional Activities at http://elt.thomson.com/gic

Internet Activities encourage students to use technology to explore a wealth of online resources.

Grammar in Context Student Book Supplements

Audio Program

- Audio CDs and Audio Tapes allow students to listen to every reading in the book as well as selected dialogs.

More Grammar Practice Workbooks

- Workbooks can be used with *Grammar in Context* or any skills text to learn and review the essential grammar.
- Great for in-class practice or homework.
- Includes practice on all grammar points in *Grammar in Context*.

Teacher's Annotated Edition

- New component offers page-by-page answers and teaching suggestions.

Assessment CD-ROM with ExamView® Pro Test Generator

- Test Generator allows teachers to create tests and quizzes quickly and easily.

Interactive CD-ROM

- CD-ROM allows for supplemental interactive practice on grammar points from *Grammar in Context*.

Split Editions

- Split Editions provide options for short courses.

Instructional Video

- Video offers teaching suggestions and advice on how to use *Grammar in Context*.

Web Site

- Web site gives access to additional activities and promotes the use of the Internet.

Toolbox

- A Toolbox available WebTutor™ on WebCT™ and Blackboard® provides chapter-by-chapter quizzes and support.

GRAMMAR

The Present Tense of the Verb *Be*
Prepositions of Place
This, That, These, Those

CONTEXT: College Life

Community College Life in the U.S.
Letter from College
Instant Message from a Student in the U.S.
In the School Cafeteria

Before You Read

Circle *T* for True or *F* for False and discuss your answers.

1. Most of the students in my class are immigrants.   T   F

2. My school is in a convenient[1] location.   T   F

Read the following article. Pay special attention to *is, am, are*.

A community college (or two-year college) **is** a good place to begin your education in the U.S. The tuition **is** usually cheaper than at a university. Because a community college **is** often smaller than a university, foreign students **are** often more comfortable. They **are** closer to their professors and get more attention.

Truman College **is** a typical community college. It **is** one of seven City Colleges of Chicago. It **is** a two-year college on the north side of Chicago. It **is** near public transportation—buses and trains—so it **is** convenient for everyone. For students with a car, parking **is** free. Credit classes **are** $70 per credit hour. Adult education classes **are** free.

Truman College **is** an international school. Many of the students **are** from other countries and **are** in ESL courses. Some of the students **are** immigrants. Some of the students **are** international students. International students **are** in the U.S. only to study. Tuition for international students **is** much higher.

Many of the students have jobs, so evening and weekend classes **are** convenient for these students. Some students have small children, so Truman has a child-care center.

The semester **is** 16 weeks long. Summer semester **is** eight weeks long. Students **are** free to choose their own classes.

---

[1]Something that is *convenient* is easy for you. A convenient location is near your house or near public transportation. Convenient classes are at a time that is good for you.

🎧 Read the following student composition. Pay special attention to *is, am, are*.

> My name **is** Rolando Lopez. I **am** from Guatemala. I **am** a student at Truman College. My major **is** engineering. I **am** married, and I work during the day. My classes **are** at night and on Saturdays. The college **is** a good place for me to start my education in the U.S. because the tuition **is** low and the attention to students **is** very high. My plan **is** to take 60 credit hours here and then go to a four-year college, such as the University of Illinois. I like it here because the teachers **are** friendly and helpful and the students from other countries **are** interesting.

1.1 | Forms of *Be*

Examples			Explanation
Subject	**Form of *Be***	**Complement**	Use *am* with *I*.
I	**am**	a college student.	
My teacher		an American.	Use *is* with *he, she, it,* and singular subjects (*teacher, wife, college*).
He		friendly.	
Truman	**is**	a City College.	
It		in Chicago.	
My wife		a student.	
She		busy.	
We		students.	Use *are* with *we, you, they,* and plural subjects.
You	**are**	the teacher.	
The students		from all over the world.	
They		immigrants.	

EXERCISE 1 Fill in the blanks with *is, are,* or *am*.

EXAMPLE My name _____*is*_____ Rolando Lopez.

1. I _____ from Guatemala.

2. My wife _____ from Mexico.

3. My wife and I _____ students.

4. The University of Illinois _____ a four-year college.

5. My classmates _____ from many different countries.

6. We _____ immigrants.

7. The professors at my college _____ friendly and helpful.

8. My major _____ engineering.

9. The semester _____ 16 weeks long.

1.2 | Uses of *Be*

Examples	Explanation
The college is **good**. Evening classes are **convenient** for me. The tuition is **low**. The teachers are very **friendly**.	Use a form of *be* with a description of the subject.
Truman College is **a community college**. The University of Illinois is **a four-year college**.	Use a form of *be* with a classification or definition of the subject.
Truman College is **in Chicago**. Chicago is **in Illinois**. The college is **near public transportation**.	Use a form of *be* with the location of the subject.
I am **from Guatemala**. My wife is **from Mexico**.	Use a form of *be* with the place of origin of the subject.
I am **24 years old**. My teacher is **about 40 years old**.	Use a form of *be* with the age of the subject.
It is **cold** in Chicago in the winter. It is **warm** in Guatemala all year.	Use *is* with weather. The subject is *it*.
It is **6 o'clock** now. It is **late**.	Use *is* with time. The subject is *it*.

EXERCISE 2 Fill in the blanks to make true statements.

EXAMPLE Chicago is _____*in Illinois*_____.
(location)

1. Chicago is a _____. Illinois is a state.
(classification)

2. My college is _____ public transportation.
(location)

3. The teacher is about _____ years old.
(age)

4. The teacher is from _____.
(place of origin)

5. It is _____ now.
(time)

6. It is _____ today.
(weather)

7. This city is _____.
(description)

1.3 | Word Order with *Be*

Examples			Explanation
Subject	***Be***	**Complement**	• The subject is first. The subject tells who or what we are talking about.
I	am	from Guatemala.	• The verb (*am, is, are*) is second.
Guatemala	is	in Central America.	• The complement is third. The complement finishes, or completes, the sentence with a location, classification, description, etc.
It	is	a small country.	
Spanish	is	my native language.	
You	are	from Vietnam.	
It	is	in Asia.	

EXERCISE 3   Put the words in the correct order to make a statement. Use a capital letter at the beginning and a period at the end.

EXAMPLE   a two-year college / my college / is   *My college is a two-year college.*

1. am / I / a student _____

2. my parents / in Guatemala / are _____

3. high / is / tuition at a four-year college _____

4. is / convenient / my college _____

5. my teacher / is / 40 years old _____

6. is / from New York / my teacher _____

7. eight weeks long / the summer semester / is _____

8. Rolando / married / is _____

1.4 | The Subject

Examples	Explanation
I am from Guatemala. **You** are an American citizen. **It** is warm in Guatemala. **We** are happy in the U.S.	The subject pronouns are: *I, you, he, she, it, we, they.*
Chicago is very big. **It** is in Illinois. **My wife** is a student. **She** is from Mexico. **My teacher** is American. **She** is a native speaker of English. **My parents** are in Guatemala. **They** are happy. **My wife and I** are in the U.S. **We** are in Chicago.	• Subject pronouns (*it, she, he, we*) can take the place of nouns (*Chicago, sister, father, friend, I*) • A noun can be singular (*my father*) or plural (*my parents*). A plural noun usually ends in *s*. • When the subject is "another person and I," put the other person before *I*. **Note:** In conversation you sometimes hear "me and my wife" in the subject position. This is very informal.
My classmates are from many countries. **They** are immigrants. **English and math** are my favorite subjects. **They** are useful subjects.	We use *they* for plural people and things.
The U.S. is a big country. **It** is in North America.	*The United States* (*the U.S.*) is a singular noun. Use *the* before United States or U.S.
You are a good teacher. **You** are good students.	*You* can be a singular or plural subject.
It is cold in Chicago in the winter. **It** is 6 o'clock now.	Use *it* to talk about time and weather.

EXERCISE **4** Fill in the blanks with the correct pronoun.

EXAMPLE Nicaragua and Guatemala are countries. ___*They*___ are in Central America.

1. My wife and I are students. _____ are at Truman College.

2. Guatemala is a small country. _____ is south of Mexico.

3. Some of the students in my class are international students. _____ are from China, Japan, and Spain.

4. _____ am a busy person.

5. English is a hard language. _____ is necessary in the U.S.

6. Adult classes at my college are free. _____ are for ESL students.

7. My book is new. _____ is *Grammar in Context*.

8. My parents are in Guatemala. _____ are old.

9. My teacher is a nice woman. _____ is from Boston.

10. My classmates and I are interested in American life. _____ are new in this country.

LETTER FROM COLLEGE

Before You Read

Circle *T* for True or *F* for False and discuss your answers.

1. The students in this class are from the same country.   T   F

2. Most of the students in this class are the same age.   T   F

Read the following letter. Pay special attention to contractions with *am, is, are*.

Dear Ola,

College **is** so different here. Students in my class **are** all ages. **We're** 22—**that's** a normal age for college students back home. But some students here **are** in their 50s or 60s. One man in my class **is** 74. **He's** from Korea. This **is** very strange for me, but it **is** interesting too. Some students **are** married. Most students have jobs, so **we're** all very busy.

The students **are** from all over the world. One student **is** from Puerto Rico. Her native language **is** Spanish, but Puerto Rico **isn't** a foreign country and it **isn't** a state of the U.S. It **is** a special territory. It **is** a small island near the U.S.

United States

Atlantic Ocean

Gulf of Mexico

Puerto Rico

(continued)

The Present Tense of the Verb *Be*; Preposition of Place; *This, That, These, Those*   **7**

The classrooms **are** different here too. **They're** big and comfortable. But the desks **are** so small. Another strange thing **is** this: The desks **are** in a circle, not in rows.

In our country, **education's** free. But here **it's** so expensive. At my college, the **tuition's** $125 per credit hour. And books **are** expensive too.

The teacher's young and informal. **He's** about my age. His **name's** Rich Weiss, and **he's** very friendly. **We're** always welcome in his office after class. But English **is** so hard. **It's** not hard to read English, but **it's** hard to understand American speech.

I'm in Minneapolis. **It's** in the northern part of the U.S. **It's** very cold here in the winter. But the summers **are** warm and sunny.

Tell me about your life. **Are** you happy with your college classes? **What's** your major now? **How's** the weather? **What's** your favorite class this semester? How are your teachers? **Are** they strict?

Take care,
Maya

1.5 | Contractions with *Be*

Examples		Explanation
I am	**I'm** in Minneapolis.	We can make a **contraction** with a subject pronoun and *am, is,* and *are.* We take out the first letter of *am, is, are* and put an apostrophe (') in its place. We usually use a contraction when we speak. We sometimes write a contraction in informal writing.
You are	**You're** a student of English.	
She is	**She's** a young teacher.	
He is	**He's** 75 years old.	
It is	**It's** cold in winter.	
We are	**We're** so busy.	
They are	**They're** big.	
The United States is a big country. Coll<u>ege</u> is different here. Engli<u>sh</u> is the language of the U.S. Ri<u>ch</u> is my English teacher.		We don't make a contraction with *is* if the noun ends in these sounds: *s, z, g, sh,* or *ch.*
Books are expensive. **The classrooms are** big.		We don't make a contraction with a plural noun and *are.*

EXERCISE 5 Fill in the blanks with the correct form of *be* (*am, is, are*). Make a contraction whenever possible. Not every sentence can have a contraction.

EXAMPLE The United States ___*is*___ a big country. It___*'s*___ between Canada and Mexico.

1. Puerto Rico _____ an island. Puerto Ricans _____ American citizens.

2. English _____ the main language of the U.S. Spanish and English _____ the languages of Puerto Rico.

3. My classmates and I _____ immigrants. We _____ in the U.S.

4. Maya _____ in Minneapolis. She _____ at a city college there.

5. Minneapolis _____ a big city. It _____ in the northern part of the U.S.

6. The teacher _____ informal. He _____ friendly.

7. The students _____ from all over the world. They _____ nice people.

8. The classroom _____ on the first floor. It _____ big.

EXERCISE 6 Fill in the blanks. Make a contraction whenever possible. Not every sentence can have a contraction.

I __*'m*___ a student of English at Truman College. _____'m
(example) (1)

happy in the U.S. My teacher _____ American. His
(2)

name _____ Charles Madison. Charles _____ an
(3) (4)

experienced teacher. _____ patient with foreign students.
(5)

My class _____ big. _____ interesting. All the students
(6) (7)

_____ immigrants, but we _____ from many different
(8) (9)

countries. Five students _____ from Asia. One woman _____
(10) (11)

from Poland. _____ from Warsaw, the capital of Poland. Many
(12)

students _____ from Mexico.
(13)

We _____ ready to learn English, but English _____ a
(14)   (15)

difficult language. I sometimes tell Charles, "You _____ a very kind
(16)

teacher." Charles says, "_____ all good students, and I _____
(17)   (18)

happy to teach you English."

1.6 | *Be* with Descriptions

Examples	Explanation
Subject *Be* (*Very*) Adjective My teacher is **young.** The desks are *very* **small.** The weather is **cold** in winter.	After a form of *be*, we can use a word that describes the subject. Descriptive words are **adjectives.** *Very* can come before an adjective.
The school is **big.** The classrooms are **big.**	Descriptive adjectives have no plural form. *Wrong:* The classrooms are bigs.
Some of my classmates are **married.** My class is **interesting.** I'm **interested** in American life.	Some words that end with –*ed* and –*ing* are adjectives: *married, divorced, worried, tired, interested, interesting, bored, boring.*
It's **cold.** I'm **thirsty.** We're **afraid.**	We use a form of *be* with physical or mental conditions: hungry, thirsty, cold, hot, tired, happy, etc.

EXERCISE 7 Complete each statement with a subject and the correct form of *be*. Write a contraction wherever possible. Make a *true* statement. Use both singular and plural subjects.

EXAMPLES   <u>My parents are</u> intelligent.   <u>The teacher's very</u> patient.

1. _____ expensive.
2. _____ cheap.
3. _____ new.
4. _____ big.
5. _____ wonderful.
6. _____ difficult.
7. _____ beautiful.
8. _____ famous.

EXERCISE 8 Write a form of *be* and an adjective to describe each of the following nouns. You may work with a partner.

EXAMPLES This classroom *is clean.* _____

New York City *is interesting.* _____

1. The teacher _____

2. This city _____

3. This college _____

4. Today's weather _____

5. Americans _____

6. American food _____

7. The students in this class _____

1.7 | *Be* with Definitions

Examples				Explanation
Singular Subject	*Be*	*A/An*	**Singular Noun**	We use a noun after a form of *be* to classify or define the subject.
I	**am**	a	student.	Use *a* or *an* before the definition of a singular noun. Use *a* before a consonant sound. Use *an* before a vowel sound. (The vowels are *a, e, i, o, u*.)
You	**are**	a	teacher.	
Puerto Rico	**is**	an	island.	
Plural Subject	*Be*		**Plural Noun**	Don't use *a* or *an* before the definition of a plural noun.
You and I	**are**		students.	*Wrong: You and I are a students.*
They	**are**		Americans.	
Subject	*Be*	*(A)*	**Adjective Noun**	We can include an adjective as part of the definition.
Chicago	is	a	**big** city.	
We	are		**good** students.	

EXERCISE 9 Fill in the blanks with a form of *be* and a definition of the subject. You may add an adjective. Be careful to add *a* or *an* for singular nouns.

EXAMPLE   California *is a state.* _____

1. Canada _____
2. Chicago _____
3. Blue _____
4. Wednesday _____
5. The Pacific and the Atlantic _____
6. White and green _____
7. January and February _____

EXERCISE 10 Add an adjective to each statement. Be careful to use *a* before a consonant and *an* before a vowel sound.

EXAMPLE   July 4 is a holiday.
July 4 is an important holiday.

1. August is a month.
2. Puerto Rico is an island.
3. A rose is a flower.
4. I'm a student.
5. Los Angeles and Chicago are cities.
6. John is a name.

EXERCISE 11 Fill in the blanks with the correct form of *be*. Add *a* or *an* for singular nouns only. Don't use an article with plural nouns.

EXAMPLES   The U.S. ____*is a*____ big country.

The U.S. and Canada ____*are*____ big countries.

1. English and Spanish _____ languages.
2. England and Spain _____ countries.
3. The University of Illinois _____ state university.
4. It _____ old university.
5. Chicago _____ interesting city.
6. Chicago and Minneapolis _____ big cities.
7. I _____ student.
8. You _____ English teacher.
9. Some students _____ immigrants.

EXERCISE 12 Complete each statement. Give a subject and the correct form of *be*. Add *a* or *an* for singular nouns only. Don't use an article with plural nouns. You may work with a partner.

EXAMPLES   *Russia is a* big country.

    Canada and Brazil are big countries.

1. _____ nice person.

2. _____ expensive item.

3. _____ American holiday.

4. _____ warm months.

5. _____ big cities.

6. _____ famous people.
    (NOTE: *people* is plural)

7. _____ American cars.

EXERCISE 13 Fill in the blanks to talk about this city. Make true statements. Remember to add *a* or *an* for a singular noun. You may work with a partner.

EXAMPLES   *Chez Paul is an* expensive restaurant in this city.

    January and February are cold months in this city.

1. _____ popular tourist attraction.

2. _____ big stores.

3. _____ beautiful months.

4. _____ beautiful park.

5. _____ inexpensive restaurant.

6. _____ busy streets.

7. _____ good college.

EXERCISE 14 Fill in the blanks to make true statements about the U.S. or another country.

EXAMPLES   *Rock music is* popular *in the U.S.*

    Politicians are rich *in my native country.*

1. _____ the biggest city _____.

2. _____ the language(s) _____.

3. _____ a popular sport _____.

4. _____ a common last name _____.

5. _____ a beautiful place _____.

The Present Tense of the Verb *Be*; Preposition of Place; *This, That, These, Those*   **13**

1.8 | Prepositions

We use prepositions to show location and origin.

Preposition	Examples
On	The book is **on** the table. The cafeteria is **on** the first floor.
At (a general area)	I am **at** school. My brother is **at** home. They are **at** work.
In (a complete or partial enclosure)	The students are **in** the classroom. The wastebasket is **in** the corner.
In front of	The blackboard is **in front of** the student.
In back of / Behind	The teacher is **in back of** the desk. The blackboard is **behind** the teacher.
Between	The empty desk is **between** the two students.
Over / Above	The exit sign is **over** the door. The clock is **above** the exit sign.
Below / Under	The textbook is **below** the desk. The dictionary is **under** the textbook.
By / Near / Close to	The pencil sharpener is **by** the window. The pencil sharpener is **near** the window. The pencil sharpener is **close to** the window.
Next to	The light switch is **next to** the door.
Far from	Los Angeles is **far from** New York.

(continued)

Preposition	Examples
Across from	Room 202 is **across from** Room 203.
In (a city)	The White House is **in** Washington, D.C.
On (a street)	The White House is **on** Pennsylvania Avenue.
At (an address)	The White House is **at** 1600 Pennsylvania Avenue.
From	Mario is **from** Brazil. He is **from** São Paolo.

EXERCISE 15   ABOUT YOU   Use a form of *be* and a preposition to tell the location of these things or people in your classroom or school.

EXAMPLE   My dictionary
My dictionary is in my book bag.

1. My classroom
2. I
3. The library
4. The cafeteria
5. The parking lot
6. The teacher
7. We
8. My books

1.9 | Negative Statements with *Be*

Examples	Explanation
I am **not** married. Peter is **not** at home. We are **not** doctors.	We put *not* after a form of *be* to make a negative statement.
I'm not late. English **isn't** my native language. My friends **aren't** here now.	We can make contractions for the negative.

Language Note: There is only one contraction of *I am not*. There are two negative contractions for all the other combinations. Study the negative contractions:

I am not	I'm not	—
you are not	you're not	you aren't
he is not	he's not	he isn't
she is not	she's not	she isn't
it is not	it's not	it isn't
we are not	we're not	we aren't
they are not	they're not	they aren't
Tom is not	Tom's not	Tom isn't

Fill in the blanks with a pronoun and a negative verb. Practice using both negative forms.

EXAMPLE   The classroom is clean and big.

_____*It isn't*_____ dirty. _____*It's not*_____ small.

1. We're in the classroom.

   _____ in the library. _____ in the cafeteria.

2. Today's a weekday.

   _____ Saturday. _____ Sunday.

3. I'm a student. _____ a teacher.

4. The students are busy.

   _____ lazy. _____ tired.

5. You're on time.

   _____ early. _____ late.

6. My classmates and I are in an English class.

   _____ in the cafeteria. _____ in the library.

EXERCISE 17   ABOUT YOU Fill in the blanks with a form of *be* to make a true affirmative statement or negative statement.

EXAMPLES   I _____*am*_____ busy on Saturdays.

My English class _____*isn't*_____ in the morning.

1. My class _____ small.

2. The students _____ all the same age.

3. The students _____ from many countries.

4. Books in the U.S. _____ expensive.

5. The teacher _____ from my native country.

6. The seats in this class _____ in a circle.

7. I _____ a full-time student.

8. My classes _____ easy.

9. We _____ in the computer room now.

EXERCISE 18   True or False. Tell if you think the following statements are true or false. Discuss your opinions.

	True	False
1. English is easy for me.		
2. English is easy for children.		
3. American teachers are very strict.[2]		
4. This school is in a nice area.		
5. This course is expensive.		
6. All Americans are rich.		
7. Baseball is popular in the U.S.		
8. January and February are nice months.		

EXERCISE 19   ABOUT YOU If you are from another country, tell your classmates about life there. Fill in the blanks with a form of *be* to make an affirmative or negative statement.

EXAMPLES   I _____'m_____ from the capital city.

I _____'m not_____ from a small town.

1. I _____ happy with the government of my country.

2. I _____ from the capital city.

3. American cars _____ common in my country.

4. Teachers _____ strict.

5. Most people _____ rich.

6. Gas _____ cheap.

7. Apartments _____ expensive.

8. Bicycles _____ a popular form of transportation.

9. Public transportation _____ good.

10. A college education _____ free.

11. The president (prime minister) _____ a woman.

12. My hometown _____ in the mountains.

13. My hometown _____ very big.

14. It _____ very cold in the winter in my hometown.

15. Cell phones _____ popular in my country.

[2]A *strict* teacher has a lot of rules.

EXERCISE 20 Use the words in parentheses ( ) to change each sentence into a negative statement.

EXAMPLE My teacher is American. (Canadian)

He isn't Canadian.

1. Los Angeles and Chicago are cities. (states)

   _____

2. I'm from Mexico. (the U.S.)

   _____

3. The U.S. is a big country. (Cuba)

   _____

4. We're in class now. (in the library)

   _____

5. You're an English teacher. (a math teacher)

   _____

6. Chicago and Springfield are in Illinois. (Miami)

   _____

7. January is a cold month. (July and August)

   _____

EXERCISE 21 ABOUT YOU Fill in the blanks with the affirmative or negative of the verb *be* to make a true paragraph.

My name ____*is*____ _____. I _____ from an
         (example)   *(your name)*   *(1)*

English-speaking country. I _____ a student at City College.
                            (2)

I _____ in my English class now. The class _____
    (3)   *(4)*

big. My teacher _____ a man. He/She _____ very
                 (5)   *(6)*

young. The classroom _____ very nice. It _____ clean.
                      (7)   *(8)*

My classmates _____ all very young students. We _____
               (9)   *(10)*

all from the same country. We _____ all immigrants.
                               (11)

Before You Read

1. Is your family in this city?

2. Do you communicate with your family and friends by e-mail?

Read the following instant message between Mohammad (MHD), a student in the U.S., and his brother, Ali (AL27), back home. Pay special attention to questions.

AL27: Hi, Mohammad.
MHD: Hi, Ali. **How are you?**
AL27: I'm fine.
MHD: **Where are you now?**
AL27: I'm in the college computer lab. **Are you at home?**
MHD: Yes, I am. It's late.

AL27: It's 4:15 p.m. here. **What time is it there?**
MHD: It's 1:15 a.m. here.
AL27: **Why are you still up[3]?**
MHD: I'm not sleepy.
AL27: **Why aren't you sleepy?**
MHD: I'm nervous about my test tomorrow.
AL27: **Why are you nervous?**
MHD: Because my class is very hard.
AL27: **How's college life in the U.S.? Is it very different from here?**
MHD: Yes, it is. But it's exciting for me. My new classmates are so interesting. They're from many countries and are all ages. One man in my class is very old.
AL27: **How old is he?**
MHD: He's 75.
AL27: **Are you serious?**
MHD: Of course, I'm serious. He's an interesting man and a great student.

AL27: **Where's** he from?
MHD: Korea.
AL27: All my classmates are young.
MHD: **Where are Mom and Dad?**
AL27: They're at work.
MHD: **Are they worried about me?**

(continued)

[3]To *be up* means to be awake.

AL27: A little.

MHD: **Why?**

AL27: Because there's so much freedom in the U.S.

MHD: Tell them I'm a good student. I'm on the dean's list.

AL27: **What's that?**

MHD: It's a list of students with a high grade point average.

AL27: That's great. Bye for now.

MHD: Bye.

1.10 | *Be* in *Yes/No* Questions and Short Answers

Compare statements, *yes/no* questions, and short answers.

Statement	*Yes/No* Question	Short Answer	Explanation
I am a student.	**Am I** a good student?	Yes, you are.	• In a *yes/no* question, we put *am, is, are* before the subject.
You are in bed.	**Are you** sleepy?	No, I'm not.	
He is old.	**Is he** a good student?	Yes, he is.	• We usually answer a *yes/no* question with a short answer. A short answer contains a pronoun. We don't use a contraction for a short *yes* answer. We usually use a contraction for a short *no* answer.
She is from Africa.	**Is she** from Nigeria?	No, she isn't.	
It is cold today.	**Is it** windy?	Yes, it is.	
We are here.	**Are we** late?	No, you aren't.	
They are worried.	**Are they** angry?	No, they aren't.	

Pronunciation Note: We usually end a *yes/no* question with rising intonation. Listen to your teacher pronounce the questions above.

EXERCISE 22 Answer the questions based on the last reading (the instant message).

EXAMPLES Is Ali in the U.S.?
No, he isn't.

Is Mohammad in the U.S.?
Yes, he is.

1. Are Ali's parents at work?

2. Are they worried about Mohammad?

3. Is Mohammad a good student?

4. Is it the same time in the U.S. and in Mohammad's native country?

5. Is Ali at home?

6. Are all the students in Mohammad's class from the same country?

7. Is Mohammad tired?

EXERCISE 23 ABOUT YOU Close your book. The teacher will ask you some questions. Answer with a true short answer. If the answer is negative, you may add more information.

EXAMPLE Is your book new?
Yes, it is. OR No, it isn't. It's a used book.

1. Is your hometown big?
2. Is Spanish your native language?
3. Is English hard for you?
4. Are you a citizen of the U.S.?
5. Is my pronunciation clear to you?
6. Am I a strict teacher?
7. Are all of you from the same country?
8. Are all of you the same age?

EXERCISE 24 Ask questions about this school and class with the words given. Another student will answer. Use the correct form of *be*.

EXAMPLE school / big
A: Is this school big?
B: Yes, it is.

1. it / near public transportation
2. the cafeteria / on this floor
3. it / open now
4. the library / in this building
5. it / closed now
6. this course / free
7. the textbooks / free
8. the teacher / strict
9. this room / clean
10. it / big

EXERCISE 25 Ask questions about the U.S. with the words given. Another student will answer. If no one knows the answer, ask the teacher.

EXAMPLE movie stars / rich
A: Are American movie stars rich?
B: Yes, they are. They're very rich.

1. a high school education / free
2. college books / free
3. medical care / free
4. doctors / rich
5. blue jeans / popular
6. houses / expensive
7. Americans / friendly
8. Japanese cars / popular
9. fast-food restaurants / popular
10. movie tickets / cheap

1.11 | *Wh-* Questions with *Be*

Examples				Explanation
Wh-Word	*Be*	Subject	Complement	A *wh-* question asks for information.
Where	**are**	Mom and Dad?		
Why	**are**	they	worried?	
How old	**is**	the teacher?		
Where	**is**	he	from?	
Why	**aren't**	you	sleepy?	

Question Words

Question	Answer	Meaning of Question Word
Who is your teacher? **Who** are those people?	My teacher is Rich Weiss. They're my parents.	Who = person
What is your classmate's name? **What** is that?	His name is Park. It's a cell phone.	What = thing
When is your test? **When** is the class over?	It's on Friday. It's over at 10 o'clock.	When = time
Why are they worried? **Why** aren't you in bed?	They're worried because you're alone. I'm not in bed because I'm not tired.	Why = reason
Where is your classmate from? **Where** are Mom and Dad now?	He's from Korea. They're at work.	Where = place
How is your life in the U.S.? **How** are you?	It's great! I'm fine.	How = description or health

Language Notes:

1. The *wh-* word + *is* can form a contraction: *who's, what's, when's, where's, how's, why's*
   We can't make a contraction for *which is*.
   We can't make a written contraction for a *wh-* word + *are*.

2. We usually end a *wh-* question with falling intonation. Listen to your teacher say the questions in the above boxes.

EXERCISE 26 Fill in the blanks with the correct question word and a form of *be*.

EXAMPLE _____*What's*_____ your name?
My name is Frank.

1. _____ Los Angeles?
   It's in California.

2. _____ your birthday?
   It's in June.

3. _____ your teacher?
   My teacher is Martha Simms.

4. _____ a rose?
   A rose is a flower.

5. _____ you late?
   I'm late because of traffic.

6. _____ your sisters and brothers?
   They're in my country.

7. _____ you?
   I'm fine. And you?

8. _____ the teacher's office?
   It's on the second floor.

9. _____ the restrooms?
   The restrooms are at the end of the hall.

10. _____ Labor Day in the U.S.?
    It's in September.

11. _____ we here?
    We're here because we want to learn English.

EXERCISE 27 Test your knowledge. Circle the correct answer to the following questions. The answers are at the end of the exercise. You may work with a partner.

1. Where's Dallas?
   a. in California   **b.** in Texas   **c.** in Illinois

2. When is American Independence Day?
   a. July 4   **b.** May 31   **c.** December 25

3. It's 8 a.m. in New York. What time is it in Los Angeles?
   a. 11 a.m.   **b.** 5 a.m.   **c.** 10 a.m.

4. On what day is Thanksgiving?
   a. on Friday   **b.** on Sunday   **c.** on Thursday

5. Which one of these is the name of a Great Lake?
   a. Mississippi   b. Missouri   c. Michigan

6. Where is the Statue of Liberty?
   a. in San Francisco   b. in New York City   c. in Los Angeles

7. What is the first day of summer?
   a. June 1   b. June 21   c. June 30

8. When is Labor Day in the U.S.?
   a. in May   b. in June   c. in September

9. What's the biggest state?
   a. Alaska   b. Texas   c. New York

Answers: 1b, 2a, 3b, 4c, 5c, 6b, 7b, 8c, 9a,

The United States of America

AL Alabama	HI Hawaii	MA Massachusetts	NM New Mexico	SD South Dakota
AK Alaska	ID Idaho	MI Michigan	NY New York	TN Tennessee
AZ Arizona	IL Illinois	MN Minnesota	NC North Carolina	TX Texas
AR Arkansas	IN Indiana	MS Mississippi	ND North Dakota	UT Utah
CA California	IA Iowa	MO Missouri	OH Ohio	VT Vermont
CO Colorado	KS Kansas	MT Montana	OK Oklahoma	VA Virginia
CT Connecticut	KY Kentucky	NE Nebraska	OR Oregon	WA Washington
DE Delaware	LA Louisiana	NV Nevada	PA Pennsylvania	WV West Virginia
FL Florida	ME Maine	NH New Hampshire	RI Rhode Island	WI Wisconsin
GA Georgia	MD Maryland	NJ New Jersey	SC South Carolina	WY Wyoming
				DC* District of Columbia

*The District of Columbia is not a state. Washington, D.C. is the capital of the United States.
 Note: Washinton, D.C., and Washington state are not the same.

For a map with major U.S. cities, see Appendix K.

1.12 | Comparing Statements and Questions with *Be*

Affirmative Statements and Questions

Wh-Word	*Be*	Subject	*Be*	Complement	Short Answer
		Mom and Dad	are	out.	
	Are	they		at the store?	No, they aren't.
Where	are	they?			
		It	is	late.	
	Is	it		1 a.m.?	No, it isn't.
What time	is	it?			

Negative Statements and Questions

Wh-Word	*Be* + n't	Subject	*Be* + n't	Complement
		You	aren't	in bed.
Why	aren't	you		sleepy?
		He	isn't	in the U.S.
Why	isn't	he		with his parents?

EXERCISE 28 Respond to each statement with a question.

EXAMPLE Mom and Dad are not here. Where *are they?*

1. Mom and Dad are worried about you. Why _____
2. I'm not sleepy. Why _____

3. My teacher is great. Who _____
4. My classes are early. When _____
5. My roommate's name is hard to pronounce.
   What _____
6. My cell phone isn't on. Why _____
7. Mom isn't in the kitchen. Where _____

1.13 | Questions with *What* and *How*

Examples	Explanation

What is a verb?
    It's an action word.
What is the Dean's List?
    It's a list of the best students.
	What can ask for a definition.

What nationality is the teacher?
    She's American.
What day is today?
    It's Friday.
What time is it?
    It's 4:15 p.m.
What color is the dictionary?
    It's yellow.
What kind of book is this?
    It's a grammar book.
	A noun can follow *what:*
	• *what nationality*
	• *what day*
	• *what time*
	• *what color*
	• *what kind (of)*
	• *what month*

How is your new class?
    It's great.
How is the weather today?
    It's cool.
	We can use *how* to ask for a description.
	
	We use *how* to ask about the weather.

How old is your brother?
    He's 16 (years old).
How tall are you?
    I'm 5 feet, 3 inches tall.
How long is this course?
    It's 16 weeks long.
How long is the table?
    It's 3 feet long.
How much is the college tuition?
    It's $75 per credit hour.
	An adjective or adverb can follow *how:*
	• *how old*
	• *how tall*
	• *how long*
	• *how much*
	• *how big*
	• *how fast*

Usage Notes:
1. For height, Americans use feet (') and inches (").
   He's 5 feet, 8 inches tall. OR He's five-eight. OR He's 5'8".[4]
2. *How are you?* is often just a way to say hello. People usually answer, "Fine, thanks. How are you?"

---

[4]See Appendix G for conversion from feet and inches to centimeters.

EXERCISE **29** Fill in the blanks to complete the questions.

EXAMPLE How _____*old are*_____ your parents? They're in their 50s.

1. What _____ it? It's 3 o'clock.

2. What _____ car _____ that?
   That's a Japanese car.

3. What _____ words _____ *tall*, *old*,
   new, and *good*? They're adjectives.

4. What _____ your new car? It's dark blue.

5. How _____? My son is 10 years old.

6. How _____? My brother is 6 feet tall.

7. How _____? I'm 25 years old.

8. How _____? That car is $10,000.

9. How _____? The movie is 2 ½ hours long.

EXERCISE **30** ABOUT YOU Fill in the blanks to make true statements about
yourself. Then find a partner from a different country, if possible,
and interview your partner by asking questions with the words in
parentheses ( ).

EXAMPLE I'm from _____*Bosnia*_____. (Where)

A: I'm from Bosnia. Where are you from?
B: I'm from Taiwan.

1. My name is _____. (What)

2. I'm from _____. (Where)

3. The president / prime minister of my country is _____
   _____. (Who)

4. The flag from my country is _____. (What colors)

5. My country is in _____. (Where)
   _____(continent or region)_____

6. I'm _____ feet, _____ inches tall. (How tall)

7. My birthday is in _____. (When)
   _____(month)_____

8. My favorite TV show is _____. (What)

EXERCISE 32 Complete the following phone conversation between Cindy (C) and Maria (M).

C: Hello?

M: Hi, Cindy. This is Maria.

C: Hi, Maria. _____How are you_____?
                    (example)

M: I'm fine.

C: _____ your first day of class?
              (1)

M: Yes, it is. I'm at school now, but I'm not in class.

C: Why _____ in class?
              (2)

M: Because it's break time now.

C: How _____ the break?
              (3)

M: It's 10 minutes long.

C: How _____ ?
              (4)

M: My English class is great. My classmates are very interesting.

C: Where _____ from?
                (5)

M: They're from all over the world.

C: _____ American?
          (6)

M: Yes. My teacher is American. What time _____?
                                                    (7)

C: It's 3:35.

M: Oh, I'm late.

C: Let's get together soon. _____ free this weekend?
                                      (8)

M: I'm free on Saturday afternoon.

C: I have a class on Saturday.

M: When _____ free?
                (9)

C: How about Sunday afternoon?

M: Sunday's fine. Talk to you later.

1. Do you like American food?

2. Do you eat in the school cafeteria?

Read the following conversation between an American (A) student and his Chinese (C) roommate. Pay special attention to *this, that, these, those.*

A: Is **this** your first time in an American college?

C: Yes, it is.

A: Let me show you around the cafeteria. **This** is the cafeteria for students. **That's** the cafeteria for teachers. The vending machines are in **that** room. When the food service is closed, **that** room is always open.

C: The food is in a machine?

A: Yes. And **that's** the change machine. **This** is the line for hot food.

C: What are **those?**

A: They're tacos.

C: **Tacos?** What are **tacos?**

A: They're Mexican food.

C: What's **that?**

A: It's pizza. It's Italian food.

C: What's **this?**

A: It's chop suey. It's a Chinese dish.

C: I'm from China, and I'm sure **this** is not a Chinese dish. Where's the American food in America?

A: This *is* American food—Mexican, Italian, Chinese—it's all American food.

C: Where are the chopsticks?

A: Uh . . . chopsticks? **Those** are the forks and knives, but there are no chopsticks here.

1.14 | *This, That, These, Those*

Examples	Explanation
Singular **This** is pizza. **Plural** **These** are tacos.	Use *this* and *these* to identify near objects and people.
Singular **That** is the change machine. **Plural** **Those** are forks and knives.	Use *that* and *those* to identify far objects and people.
This is pizza. **It's** an Italian food. **Those** are knives and forks. **They're** clean. **That's** my teacher. **She's** a nice woman.	After we identify a noun, we can use subject pronouns.
That room is for the teachers. **Those forks** are clean.	A noun can follow *this, that, these, those*.

Language Note: Only *that is* can form a contraction in writing: **That's** the change machine.

EXERCISE 32 Imagine that you are showing a new student the school cafeteria. Use *this*, *that*, *these*, and *those*, and a form of *be* to complete each statement. The arrows indicate if the item is near or far.

EXAMPLES _____*This is*_____ the school cafeteria. →

_____*Those are*_____ the clean dishes. ⟶

1. _____ the trays. →

2. _____ today's special. →

3. _____ the napkins. →

4. _____ the forks, knives, and spoons. ⟶

5. _____ the cashier. →

6. _____ the vending machines. ⟶

7. _____ the eating area. ⟶

8. _____ the teachers' section. ⟶

1. Uses of *Be*

DESCRIPTION:	Chicago **is** big.
IDENTIFICATION / CLASSIFICATION:	This **is** Chicago. It **is** a city.
LOCATION:	Chicago **is** in Illinois.
PLACE OF ORIGIN:	The teacher **is** from Chicago.
AGE:	I **am** 25 (years old).
PHYSICAL OR MENTAL CONDITION:	He **is** hungry. I **am** thirsty. She **is** worried.
TIME:	It **is** 6 p.m.
WEATHER:	It **is** warm today.

2. Subject Pronouns

    I   we   he   she   it   you   they

3. Contractions

    Subject pronoun + form of *be:* I'm, you're, he's, she's, it's, we're, they're

    Subject noun + *is:* the teacher's, Tom's, Mary's

    Is or *are* + *not:* isn't, aren't

    Wh- word + *is:* what's, when's, where's, why's, how's

4. *This / That / These / Those*

    This is an English book.
    These are pencils.
    That is a pen.
    Those are pens.

5. Articles *a / an*

    Chicago is **a** big city.
    Puerto Rico is **an** island.

6. Statements and Questions with *Be*

AFFIRMATIVE:	She **is** busy.
NEGATIVE:	She **isn't** lazy.
YES/NO QUESTION:	Is she busy on Saturday?
SHORT ANSWER:	No, she **isn't.**
WH- QUESTION:	When **is** she busy?
NEGATIVE QUESTION:	Why **isn't** she busy on Saturday?
AFFIRMATIVE:	You **are** late.
NEGATIVE:	You **aren't** on time.
YES/NO QUESTION:	**Are** you OK?
SHORT ANSWER:	Yes, I **am.**
WH- QUESTION:	Why **are** you late?
NEGATIVE QUESTION:	Why **aren't** you on time?

1. Don't repeat the subject with a pronoun.

   My father ~~he~~ lives in Australia.

2. Use correct word order. Put the subject at the beginning of the statement.

   Cuba is small.
   ~~Is small Cuba.~~

3. Use the correct word order. Put the adjective before the noun.

   small country.
   Cuba is a ~~country small.~~

4. Use the correct word order in a question.

   is he
   Where ~~he is~~ from?

5. Every sentence has a verb. Don't omit *be*.

   is
   My sister ˄ a teacher.

6. Every sentence has a subject. For time and weather, the subject is *it*.

   It's
   ~~Is~~ 6 o'clock now.
   It's
   ~~Is~~ very cold today.

7. Don't confuse *your* (possession) with *you're*, the contraction for *you are*.

   You're
   ~~Your~~ a good teacher.

8. Don't confuse *this* and *these*.

   This
   ~~These~~ is my coat.
   These
   ~~This~~ are my shoes.

9. The plural of the subject pronoun *it* is *they*, not *its*.

   They're
   Dogs are friendly animals. ~~Its~~ good pets.

10. Use *the* before *U.S.* and *United States*.

    the
    My sister is in ˄ U.S.

11. Use a singular verb after *the U.S.*

    The U.S. ~~are~~ *is* a big country.

12. Do not use a contraction for *am not.*

    ~~I amn't~~ *I'm not* an American.

13. Put the apostrophe in place of the missing letter.

    She ~~is'nt~~ *isn't* here today.

14. Use an apostrophe, not a comma, for a contraction.

    ~~I,m~~ *I'm* a good student.

15. Use the article *a* or *an* before a singular noun.

    New York is *a* big city.

    San Francisco is *an* interesting city.

16. Don't use *a* before plural nouns.

    July and August are ~~a~~ warm months.

17. Don't use the article *a* before an adjective with no noun.

    New York is ~~a~~ big.

18. Use *an* before a vowel sound.

    Puerto Rico is ~~a~~ *an* island.

19. Don't make an adjective plural.

    My daughters are beautiful~~s~~.

20. Don't make a contraction with *is* after *s, z, sh,* or *ch* sounds.

    Los Angeles~~'s~~ *is* a big city.

21. For age, use a number only or a number + *years old.*

    He's 12 ~~years.~~ OR *He's 12 years old.*

22. Don't use a contraction for a short *yes* answer.

    Are you from Mexico? Yes, ~~I'm~~ *I am*.

23. Don't separate *how* from the adjective or adverb.

    How ~~is he old?~~ *old is he?*

PART 1 Find the mistakes with the underlined words and correct them. Not every sentence has a mistake. If the sentence is correct, write *C*.

EXAMPLES   ~~He,s~~ my brother.   *He's*

Chicago's a big city.   *C*

1. New York and Los Angeles are <u>a big cities.</u>

2. The <u>teacher's</u> not here today.

3. She <u>is'nt</u> in the library.

4. I <u>amn't</u> from Pakistan. <u>I'm</u> from India.

5. <u>The students they</u> are very smart.

6. We are <u>intelligents</u> students.

7. <u>We're</u> not hungry. We <u>aren't</u> thirsty.

8. <u>It's</u> warm today.

9. <u>I'm</u> from Ukraine. My <u>wife from</u> Poland.

10. My little brother <u>is 10 years.</u>

11. <u>French's</u> a beautiful language.

12. <u>It's</u> 4:35 now.

13. <u>Your</u> in the U.S. now.

14. <u>These</u> is a good book.

15. <u>These</u> are my pencils.

16. Those dogs are beautiful. <u>Its</u> friendly.

17. I live in <u>U.S.</u>

18. January is <u>cold month.</u>

19. My father is <u>a tall.</u>

20. New York City and Los Angeles are <u>bigs.</u>

21. This is <u>a</u> interesting book.

22. Is he from Peru? Yes, <u>he's.</u>

23. Chicago <u>it's</u> a big city.

PART 2 Find the mistakes with word order and correct them. Not every sentence has a mistake. If the sentence is correct, write *C*.

EXAMPLES I have a book new.
She is 25 years old. *C*

1. Is very long this book.

2. She has a car very beautiful.

3. Why you are late?

4. How old are you?

5. What nationality your wife is?

6. What color is your new coat?

7. Why the teacher is absent?

8. Is your father a doctor?

PART 3 Fill in the blanks to complete this conversation. Not all blanks need a word. If the blank doesn't need a word, write Ø.

A: Where are you ___*from*___?
(example)

B: I'm from ___Ø___ Mexico.
(example)

A: Are you happy in _____ U.S.?
(1)

B: Yes. I _____. The U.S. is _____ great country.
(2)   (3)

A: _____ from _____ big city?
(4)   (5)

B: Yes. I'm from Mexico City. It's _____ very big city. This city is
(6)

_____ big and beautiful too. But _____ cold in the winter.
(7)   (8)

A: _____ from Mexico too?
(9)

B: No, my roommate _____ from Taiwan. I'm happy in the
(10)

U.S., but he _____ happy here.
(11)

A: Why _____ happy?
(12)

The Present Tense of the Verb *Be*; Preposition of Place; *This, That, These, Those*   **35**

B: He _____ homesick. His parents _____ in Taiwan.
(13)   (14)

He _____ alone here.
(15)

A: How _____ ?
(16)

B: He's very young. He _____ only 18 years _____ .
(17)   (18)

A: What _____ his name?
(19)

B: His name _____ Lu.
(20)

PART 4 Write a contraction of the words shown. If it's not possible to make a contraction, put an *X* in the blank.

EXAMPLES she is ___*she's*___

English is ___*X*___

1. we are _____
2. you are not _____
3. I am not _____
4. they are _____
5. this is _____

6. Los Angeles is _____
7. Mary is not _____
8. he is not _____
9. what is _____
10. what are _____

PART 5 Read the conversation between two students, Sofia (S) and Danuta (D). They are talking about their classes and teachers. Fill in the blanks.

D: Hi, Sofia. How's your English class?

S: Hi, Danuta. It___'s___ wonderful. I _____ very happy with it.
(example)   (1)

D: _____'m in level 3. What level _____ in?
(2)   (3)

S: I' _____ in level 2.
(4)

D: My English teacher _____ Ms. Kathy James. _____ a very
(5)   (6)

good teacher. Who _____ ?
(7)

S: Mr. Bob Kane is my English teacher. _____ very good, too.
(8)

D: _____ an old man?
(9)

S: No, he _____. He's _____ young man. He _____
(10)   (11)   (12)

about 25 years _____. How _____?
(13)   (14)

D: Ms. James _____ about 50 years old.
(15)

S: How _____?
(16)

D: She's about 5 feet, 6 inches tall.

S: Is she American?

D: Yes, she _____. She's from New York.
(17)

S: _____?
(18)

D: Yes. My class is very big. The students _____ from many
(19)

countries. Ten students _____ from Asia, six students
(20)

_____ from Europe, one student _____ from Africa, and
(21)   (22)

five are _____ Central America. Is your class big?
(23)

S: No, it _____.
(24)

D: Where _____?
(25)

S: The students _____ all from the same country. We _____
(26)   (27)

from Russia.

D: _____ Russian?
(28)

S: No. Mr. Kane isn't Russian. He's from Canada, but he's _____
(29)

American citizen now.

D: _____?
(30)

S: No. That's not Mr. Kane. That _____ my husband. I _____
(31) (32)

late! See you later.

EXPANSION ACTIVITIES

Classroom Activities

1. Write a few sentences about yourself. Give your height, a physical description, your nationality, your occupation, your age (optional), your gender (man or woman). Put the papers in a box. The teacher will read each paper. Guess which classmate is described.

   EXAMPLE I'm 5 feet, 8 inches tall.
   I'm Mexican.
   I'm thin.
   I'm 21 years old.

2. Work with a partner. Describe a famous person (an actor, a singer, an athlete, a politician). Report your description to the class. Do not give the person's name. See if your classmates can guess who it is.

   EXAMPLE He is a former basketball player.
   He's tall.
   He's famous.
   He's an African American.

3. Check the words that describe you. Find a partner and ask each other questions using these words. See how many things you have in common. Tell the class something interesting you learned about your partner.

   a. ____ happy

   b. ____ from Africa

   c. ____ from Asia

   d. ____ from Europe

   e. ____ interested in politics

   f. ____ a grandparent

   g. ____ under 20 years old

   h. ____ in love

   i. ____ afraid to speak English

   j. ____ an only child[5]

   k. ____ from the capital of my country

   l. ____ an American citizen

   m. ____ hungry

   n. ____ married

   o. ____ athletic

[5]An *only child* has no sisters or brothers.

4. Fill in the blanks. Then find a partner and read your sentences to your partner. See how many times you match your partner's sentence.

a. Love is _____

b. This city is _____

c. Children are _____

d. The teacher is _____

e. Money is _____

f. The American president is _____

g. My friends are _____

h. I am _____

i. Public transportation in this city is _____

j. This book is _____

5. Work with a partner from the same country, if possible. Fill in a few items for each category. Report some information to the class.

EXAMPLE   Typical of the U.S.

Common last names	Common cars	Popular tourist attractions	Popular sports	Language(s)	Capital city	Other big cities
Johnson Wilson	Ford Chevy Toyota	Disneyland Grand Canyon	baseball basketball football	English	Washington	New York Los Angeles Chicago

Typical of _____ (your country)

Common last names	Common cars	Popular tourist attractions	Popular sports	Language(s)	Capital city	Other big cities

Write About it

Write a paragraph using Exercise 21 as a model. For every negative statement that you write, add an affirmative statement. You may add other information, too.

EXAMPLE

●	*My name is Mohammad. I'm not from an English speaking country. I'm from Iran. I'm not a student at City College. I'm a student at Roosevelt University. I'm in English class now....*

Outside Activities

Interview a native speaker of English (a neighbor, a coworker, another student or a teacher at this college). Ask him or her the following questions. Report this person's answers to the class.

a. What city are you from?
b. Are your parents or grandparents from another country? Where are they from?
c. Is most of your family in this city?
d. Are you happy with this city? Why or why not?
e. What are your favorite places in this city?

Internet Activities

Using the Internet, find the Web site of a college you are interested in. Or find the Web site of the college or school you are at now. What information is on the home page? What links are on the home page?

Additional Activities at **http://elt.thomson.com/gic**

GRAMMAR
The Simple Present Tense

CONTEXT: The U.S. Government
Washington, D.C.
The IRS

The White House, Washington, D.C.

WASHINGTON, D.C.

Before You Read

1. What capital cities do you know?

2. What do you know about Washington, D.C?

The Lincoln Memorial

The Capitol

The Vietnam War Memorial

Read the following article. Pay special attention to the present-tense verbs.

Washington, D.C., **is** the capital of the United States. "D.C." **means** District of Columbia. The District of Columbia **is** not a state; it **is** a special government district. It **is** very small. It **is** only 61 square miles (158 square kilometers.) More than half a million people **live** in Washington. Washington **doesn't** have factories. Government and tourism **are** the main businesses of Washington. Washington **doesn't have** tall buildings like other big cities.

Some people who work in Washington **don't live** there. They **live** in the nearby states: Virginia and Maryland. Washington **has** a good subway (metro) system. It **connects** Washington to nearby cities in Virginia and Maryland.

The Capitol, the building where Congress **meets, is** on a hill. State senators and representatives **work** in the capital. They **make** the country's laws.

Tourists from all over the United States and many other countries **visit** Washington. They **come** to see the White House and the Capitol building. Many visitors **want** to see the Vietnam War Memorial. This wall of dark stone **lists** all the names of American soldiers who died in the war in Vietnam.

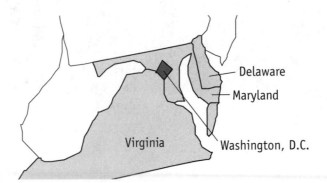

Delaware

Maryland

Virginia

Washington, D.C.

Besides government buildings, Washington also **has** many important museums and monuments to presidents. The Smithsonian Institution **has** 16 museums and galleries and a zoo. The Smithsonian **includes** the Air and Space Museum. This very popular museum **shows** visitors real spaceships, such as the Apollo 11, which landed on the moon in 1969.

Tourists **don't pay** to see government buildings and museums. However, they **need** tickets to see many places because these places are crowded. Government buildings and museums **have** a lot of security. Guards **check** visitors' bags as they **enter** these buildings.

A trip to Washington **is** an enjoyable and educational experience.

2.1 | Simple Present Tense—Forms

A simple present-tense verb has two forms: the base form and the -s form.

Examples	Explanation
Subject **Base Form** **Complement** I You We **live** in Washington. They My friends	We use the base form when the subject is *I, you, we, they,* or a plural noun.
Subject **-s Form** **Complement** He She It **lives** in Washington. The president My family	We use the -s form when the subject is *he, she, it,* or a singular noun. *Family* is a singular subject.

Washington **has** many museums.
The metro **goes** to Virginia.
The president **does** a lot of work.
	Three verbs have an irregular -s form.
	    have → has (pronunciation /hæz/)
	    go → goes
	    do → does (pronunciation /dʌz/)

EXERCISE **1** Fill in the blanks with the correct form of the verb.

EXAMPLE Visitors ____like____ the museums.
         (like/likes)

1. The president _____ in the White House.
   (live/lives)

2. Many people in Washington _____ for the government.
   (work/works)

3. Washington _____ many beautiful museums.
   (have/has)

4. Millions of tourists _____ Washington every year.
   (visit/visits)

5. The metro _____ Washington to nearby cities.
   (connect/connects)

6. The Vietnam War Memorial _____ the names of men and
   women who died in the war.   (list/lists)

7. "D.C." _____ District of Columbia.
   (mean/means)

2.2 | Simple Present Tense—Uses

Examples	Uses
The president **lives** in the White House. Washington **has** a good subway (metro) system.	With general truths, to show that something is consistently true
The president **shakes** hands with many people. He **waves** to people.	With customs
We **take** a vacation every summer. We sometimes **go** to Washington.	To show regular activity (a habit) or repeated action
I **come** from Bosnia. He **comes** from Pakistan.	To show place of origin

EXERCISE 2 ABOUT YOU Write the correct form of the verb. Add more words to give facts about you.

EXAMPLE I _____*come from Colombia*_____ .
         (come)

1. The capital of my country _____ .
                              (have)

2. Most people in my country _____ .
                              (have)

3. In my native city, I especially _____ .
                                    (like)

4. Tourists in my country _____ .
                           (visit)

5. My native city _____ .
                   (have)

6. My family _____ .
             (live)

7. In the U.S., I _____ .
                  (live)

8. The U.S. _____ .
            (have)

9. I _____ College/School.
      (attend)

10. This school _____ .
                 (have)

2.3 | Spelling of the -*s* Form

Rule	Base Form	-*s* Form
Add **s** to most verbs to make the -*s* form.	hope eat	hopes eats
When the base form ends in *ss, sh, ch,* or *x,* add **es** and pronounce an extra syllable.	miss wash catch mix	misses washes catches mixes
When the base form ends in a consonant + *y,* change the *y* to *i* and add **es.**	carry worry	carries worries
When the base form ends in a vowel + *y,* add **s.** Do not change the *y.*	pay enjoy	pays enjoys

EXERCISE 3 Write the -s form of the following verbs.

EXAMPLES   eat   *eats*

                study   *studies*

                watch   *watches*

1. try _____	11. say _____
2. play _____	12. change _____
3. have _____	13. brush _____
4. go _____	14. obey _____
5. worry _____	15. reach _____
6. finish _____	16. fix _____
7. do _____	17. work _____
8. push _____	18. raise _____
9. enjoy _____	19. charge _____
10. think _____	20. see _____

2.4 | Pronunciation of the -s Form

Pronunciation	Rule	Examples	
/s/	Pronounce /s/ after voiceless sounds: /p, t, k, f/.	hope—hopes eat—eats	pick—picks laugh—laughs
/z/	Pronounce /z/ after voiced sounds: /b, d, g, v, m, n, ŋ, l, r/ and all vowel sounds.	grab—grabs read—reads hug—hugs live—lives hum—hums run—runs	sing—sings fall—falls hear—hears see—sees borrow—borrows
/əz/	Pronounce /əz/ when the base form ends in *ss, ce, se, sh, ch, ge, x.*	miss—misses dance—dances use—uses wash—washes	watch—watches change—changes fix—fixes

Language Note: The following verbs have a change in the vowel sound. Listen to your teacher pronounce these examples.

    do/du/—does/dʌz/

    say/sei/—says/sɛz/

EXERCISE **4**   Go back to Exercise 3 and pronounce the base form and -s form of each verb.

EXERCISE **5**   Fill in the blanks with the -s form of the verb in parentheses ( ). Pay attention to the spelling rules on page 45. Then pronounce each sentence.

EXAMPLE   A teacher _____*tries*_____ to help students learn.
                                       (try)

1. A pilot _____ an airplane.
            (fly)

2. A dishwasher _____ dishes.
                  (wash)

3. A babysitter _____ children.
                  (watch)

4. A soldier _____ an officer.
              (obey)

5. A citizen _____ taxes.
              (pay)

6. A mechanic _____ machines.
                (fix)

7. A student _____.
              (study)

8. A student _____ homework.
              (do)

9. A carpenter _____ a hammer.
                (use)

10. A teacher _____ students.
               (teach)

EXERCISE **6**   Choose one of the following professions. Write at least three sentences to tell what someone in this profession does. You may work with a partner.

mechanic	teacher	bus driver
secretary	cook	tour guide
carpenter	banker	salesperson
plumber	writer	lawyer

_____

_____

_____

_____

2.5 | Comparing Affirmative Statements—*Be* and Other Verbs

Examples	Explanation
I **am** a student. I **study** English. You **are** right. You **know** the answer. He **is** busy. He **works** hard.	Don't include a form of *be* with a simple present-tense verb. *Wrong: I'm study English.* *Wrong: You're know the answer.* *Wrong: He's works hard.*

EXERCISE 7   A student is comparing himself to his friend. Fill in the blanks with the correct form of the underlined verb.

EXAMPLES   My friend and I are very different.

I get up at 7 o'clock. He ____*gets*____ up at 10.

I'm a good student. He _____*'s*_____ a lazy student.

1. I study every day. He _____ only before a test.

2. I always get A's on my tests. He _____ C's.

3. I have a scholarship. He _____ a government loan.

4. I'm a good student. He _____ an average student.

5. He lives in a dormitory. I _____ in an apartment.

6. He's from Japan. I _____ from the Philippines.

7. He studies with the radio on. I _____ in a quiet room.

8. He watches a lot of TV. I _____ TV only when I have free time.

9. He eats a lot of meat. I _____ a lot of fish.

10. He uses a laptop computer. I _____ a desktop computer.

2.6 | Negative Statements with the Simple Present Tense

Examples	Explanation
The president **lives** in the White House. The vice president **doesn't live** in the White House. Washington **has** many government buildings. It **doesn't have** tall buildings.	Use *doesn't* + the base form with *he, she, it,* or a singular noun. **Compare:** lives → doesn't **live** has → doesn't **have** *Doesn't* is the contraction for *does not.*
Visitors **pay** to enter museums in most cities. They **don't pay** in Washington museums. We **live** in Maryland. We **don't live** in Washington.	Use *don't* + the base form with *I, you, we, they,* or a plural noun. **Compare:** pay → don't **pay** live → don't **live** *Don't* is the contraction for *do not.*

Usage Note: American English and British English use different grammar to form the negative of *have.* Compare:

American: He *doesn't have* a dictionary.

British: He *hasn't* a dictionary. OR He *hasn't got* a dictionary.

EXERCISE 8 Fill in the blanks with the negative form of the underlined verb.

EXAMPLE You <u>need</u> tickets for some museums. You _____*don't need*_____ money for the museums.

1. Washington <u>has</u> tourism. It _____ factories.

2. Tourists <u>need</u> to pass through security in Washington museums.

They _____ to pay to enter a museum.

3. The metro <u>runs</u> all day. It _____ after midnight.

4. You <u>need</u> a car in many cities. You _____ a car in Washington.

5. Washington <u>has</u> a subway system (the metro). Miami _____ _____ a subway system.

6. My friend <u>lives</u> in Virginia. He _____ in Washington.

7. I <u>like</u> American history. I _____ geography.

8. The president <u>lives</u> in Washington. He _____ in New York.

9. The president <u>serves</u> for four years. He _____ for six years.

10. We <u>have</u> a president. We _____ a prime minister.

11. The U.S. Congress <u>makes</u> the laws. The president _____ the laws.

12. Many Washingtonians <u>work</u> in tourism. They _____ for the government.

EXERCISE 9 Tell if this school has or doesn't have the following items.

EXAMPLES ESL courses
This school has ESL courses.

classes for children
It doesn't have classes for children.

1. a library	5. a swimming pool	9. dormitories
2. a cafeteria	6. a gym	10. classes for children
3. copy machines	7. a student newspaper	11. a computer lab
4. a parking lot	8. a theater	12. e-mail for students

EXERCISE 10 Make an affirmative statement or a negative statement with the words given to state facts about the teacher. Use the correct form of the verb.

EXAMPLE speak Arabic
The teacher speaks Arabic.
OR
The teacher doesn't speak Arabic.

1. talk fast	6. pronounce my name correctly
2. speak English well	7. wear glasses
3. speak my language	8. wear jeans to class
4. give a lot of homework	9. teach this class every day
5. give tests	10. watch the students during a test

EXERCISE **11** ABOUT YOU Check (✓) the items that describe you and what you do. Exchange your book with another student. Make statements about the other student.

EXAMPLES   ____ I have children.   _✓_ I like cold weather.
Marta doesn't have children.   Marta likes cold weather.

1. ____ I speak Chinese.   6. ____ I like summer.

2. ____ I live alone.   7. ____ I like cold weather.

3. ____ I live near school.   8. ____ I have a laptop.

4. ____ I walk to school.   9. ____ I use the Internet.

5. ____ I speak Spanish.   10. ____ I have a dog.

2.7 | Comparing Negative Statements with *Be* and Other Verbs

Examples	Explanation
I**'m not** from Mexico. I **don't speak** Spanish.	Don't use *be* to make the negative of a simple present-tense verb.
You **aren't** sick. You **don't need** a doctor.	*Wrong:* I *am* don't speak Spanish. *Wrong:* You *aren't* need a doctor.
He **isn't** hungry. He **doesn't want** dinner.	*Wrong:* He *isn't want* dinner.

EXERCISE **12** ABOUT YOU Check (✓) the items that describe you and what you do. Exchange your book with another student. Make statements about the other student.

EXAMPLES   ____ I'm an immigrant.
Margarita isn't an immigrant. She comes from Puerto Rico.

    _✓_ I have a laptop.
Margarita has a laptop.

1. ____ I'm married.   7. ____ I'm a full-time student.

2. ____ I have children/a child.   8. ____ I have a pet.[1]

3. ____ I have a laptop.   9. ____ I'm an immigrant.

4. ____ I'm an American citizen.   10. ____ I'm happy in the U.S.

5. ____ I like this city.   11. ____ I like baseball.

6. ____ I have a job.   12. ____ I understand American TV.

[1] A *pet* is an animal that lives in someone's house. Dogs and cats are common pets.

EXERCISE 13 Choose one of the items from the list below. Write sentences telling what this person does or is. Include negative statements. You may work with a partner. Read some of your sentences to the class.

EXAMPLE a good teacher

A good teacher explains the lesson.

A good teacher doesn't get angry at students.

A good teacher doesn't walk away after class when students have

questions.

A good teacher is patient.

1. a good friend   3. a good doctor
2. a good mother or father   4. a good adult son or daughter

_____

_____

_____

_____

EXERCISE 14 Fill in the blanks with the correct form of the verb in parentheses ( ).

Sara Harris ____is____ a 30-year-old woman. She _____ in
     Example: (be)   *(1 live)*

Arlington, Virginia. She _____ in Washington because rent is
                    (2 not/live)

cheaper in Arlington. Arlington _____ far from Washington.
                          (3 be/not)

Sara _____ a car because her apartment _____ near
     (4 not/need)   *(5 be)*

a metro stop. She _____ the metro to go to work every day.
          (6 use)

Sara works in Washington, but she _____ for the government.
                 (7 not/work)

She _____ a tour guide. She _____ groups on tours of
    (8 be)   *(9 take)*

the Capitol. Tour groups _____ to pay to enter the Capitol,
              (10 not/need)

but they _____ a reservation.
     (11 need)

Sara _____ married. She _____ two
        (12 be/not)   (13 have)

roommates. They _____ in government offices. Sara and her
                        (14 work)

roommates _____ hard, so they _____ much time to
                (15 work)   (16 not/have)

visit the museums. When Sara's friends _____ from out of town,
                                                (17 visit)

Sara _____ them to museums and other tourist attractions.
        (18 take)

THE IRS

Before You Read

1. Do you pay income tax?

2. What other kinds of taxes do you pay?

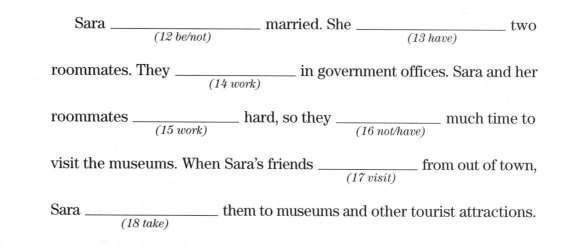

Read the following conversation between Annie (A) and Barbara
(B) in Washington, D.C. Pay special attention to questions.

A: **Do** you **live** in Washington?
B: No, I don't. I live in Virginia.
A: **Do** you **work** in Washington?
B: Yes, I do.
A: How **do** you **go** to work?
B: I use the metro.
A: How much **does** it **cost**?
B: That depends on how far you ride. I pay $1.50 per ride.
A: Where **do** you **work**?
B: I work at the IRS.

(continued)

A: What **does** IRS **mean**?

B: It means Internal Revenue Service. This is the government agency that collects taxes. Whenever I tell people that I work at the IRS, they give me funny looks or say funny things.

A: Why?

B: Because everyone hates the IRS. No one likes to pay taxes. But taxes are necessary.

A: How **does** the IRS **use** the money?

B: For the military, education, health care, social security, and many other things.

A: **Does** everyone **pay** the same amount of tax?

B: No. Poor people pay a smaller percentage. Middle income people pay more. The tax law is very complicated[2].

A: When **do** people in the U.S. **pay** tax?

B: They pay little by little. Money comes out of their paychecks. Then they fill out a form and send it to the IRS every year by April 15.

A: My friend gets a refund[3] every year. **Does** everyone **get** a refund?

B: No. Only people who pay too much during the year get a refund. If we pay too little, we send a check to the IRS by April 15.

A: I hope to win the lottery some day. Then I won't need to pay taxes.

B: You're wrong! The IRS takes a percentage from every lottery winning.

A: How **does** the IRS **know** who wins the lottery?

B: The lottery reports the winner's name to the IRS. A famous American, Benjamin Franklin, said, "In this world nothing is certain but death and taxes."

2.8 | *Yes/No* Questions and Short Answers with the Present Tense

Examples				Explanation
Does	Subject	Verb	Complement	To form a question with *he, she, it, everyone, family,* or a singular subject, use:
Does	Barbara	**work**	in Washington?	
Does	she	**live**	in Virginia?	*Does* + subject + base form
Does	everyone	**pay**	taxes?	*Wrong:* Does she *works* in Washington?
Does	your family	**visit**	you?	
Do	Subject	Verb	Complement	To form a question with *I, we, you, they,* or a plural noun, use:
Do	you	**work**	hard?	
Do	they	**pay**	taxes?	*Do* + subject + base form
Do	Americans	**like**	the IRS?	

(continued)

[2] *Complicated* means not simple.
[3] A *refund* is money that the government returns to you if you pay too much in taxes.

Examples	Explanation

Do lottery winners pay taxes?
Yes, they do.
Do Americans like taxes?
No, they don't.
Does Barbara use the metro?
Yes, she does.
Does she live in Washington?
No, she doesn't.
	We usually answer a *yes/no* question with a short answer.
	Short answer:
	    Yes, + subject pronoun + *do/does*.
	    No, + subject pronoun + *don't/doesn't*.

Usage Note: American English and British English use different grammar to form a question with *have*. Compare:

      American: Does she *have* a car? Yes, she *does*.

       British: *Has* she a car? OR *Has* she *got* a car? Yes, she *has*.

Compare Statements and Questions

Do/Does	Subject	Verb	Complement	Short Answer
	Barbara	works	in Washington.	
Does	she	work	for the government?	No, she doesn't.
	You	pay	taxes.	
Do	you	pay	a lot?	Yes, I do.

EXERCISE 15 Answer with a short answer.

EXAMPLE Does Barbara work in Washington, D.C.? _____ *Yes, she does.*

    1. Does Barbara live in Washington, D.C.? _____

    2. Does she work for the government? _____

    3. Does the Washington metro go to Virginia? _____

    4. Does tax money pay for the military? _____

    5. Do poor people pay taxes? _____

    6. Do people like to pay taxes? _____

    7. Do lottery winners pay taxes? _____

    8. Does Annie have a lot of questions for Barbara? _____

EXERCISE 16 Ask your teacher a question with "Do you . . . ?" and the words given. Your teacher will respond with a short answer.

EXAMPLE drive to school

A: Do you drive to school?
B: Yes, I do. OR No, I don't.

1. like your job
2. teach in the summer
3. have another job
4. speak another language
5. learn English from TV
6. know my language
7. like to read students' homework.
8. live far from the school
9. have a fax machine
10. have trouble with English spelling
11. have a scanner
12. like soccer

EXERCISE 17 ABOUT YOU Put a check(✓) next to customs from your native country. Then make an affirmative or negative statement about your native country or culture. Ask another student if this is a custom in his or her native country or culture.

EXAMPLE ___✓___ People take off their shoes before they enter a house.

A: Russians take off their shoes before they enter a house. Do Mexicans take off their shoes before they enter a house?
B: No, we don't.

1. _____ People take off their shoes before they enter a house.
2. _____ People bow when they say hello.
3. _____ People shake hands when they say hello.
4. _____ People bring a gift when they visit a friend's house.
5. _____ People eat with chopsticks.
6. _____ On the bus, younger people stand up to let an older person person sit down.
7. _____ High school students wear a uniform.
8. _____ People visit friends without calling first.
9. _____ Men open doors for women.
10. _____ Men give flowers to women for their birthdays.
11. _____ People celebrate children's day.
12. _____ Women cover their faces with a veil.

EXERCISE 18 A tourist in Washington, D.C., has a lot of questions. Fill in the blanks to make questions.

EXAMPLE Most big cities have tall buildings. _Does Washington have_ tall buildings?
No, it doesn't.

1. The metro trains run all day. _____ 24 hours a day?
No, they don't. They only run from early morning to midnight. On weekends they run later.

2. In my city, all passengers pay the same fare on the metro.

_____ the same fare in the metro in Washington?
No, they don't. Passengers pay according to the distance they ride.

3. I need a ticket to enter museums back home. _____

_____ ticket to enter museums in Washington?
Yes, you do, but the museums are free.

4. The Washington Monument is very tall. _____ an elevator?
Yes, it has an elevator.

5. The president works in Washington. _____ on Capitol Hill?
No, he doesn't. He works in the White House.

6. _____ the laws?
No, he doesn't. The president doesn't make the laws. Congress makes the laws.

EXERCISE 19 Two students are comparing teachers. Fill in the blanks to complete this conversation.

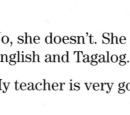

A: Do you ___*like*___ your English class?
(example: like)

B: Yes, I _____. I _____ a very good teacher.
      (1)   *(2 have)*
Her name is Ms. Lopez.

A: _____ Spanish?
                (3)

B: No, she doesn't. She comes from the Philippines. She _____
English and Tagalog.   *(4 speak)*

A: My teacher is very good too. But he _____ fast, and sometimes
                                          (5 talk)

I _____ him. He _____ a lot of homework.
  (6 not / understand)   *(7 give)*

_____ a lot of homework?
        (8)

B: Yes, she does. And she _____ a test once a week.
(9 give)

A: My teacher _____ jeans to class. He's very informal.
(10 wear)

_____ jeans to class?
(11)

B: No, she doesn't. She always wears a dress.

A: My teacher always _____ to us about American culture.
(12 talk)

_____ your teacher _____ to you about American culture?
(13)   *(14)*

B: Yes, she _____.
(15)

2.9 | Comparing *Yes/No* Questions—*Be* and Other Verbs

Examples		Explanation
Are you lost?	No, I'm not.	Don't use *be* to make a question with a simple present-tense verb.
Do you **need** help?	No, I **don't**.	
Am I right?	Yes, you **are**.	*Wrong: Are you need help?*
Do I **have** the answer?	Yes, you **do**.	*Wrong: Am I have the answer?*
Is he from Haiti?	Yes, he **is**.	*Wrong: Is he speak French?*
Does he speak French?	Yes, he **does**.	

EXERCISE 20 Read each statement. Write a *yes/no* question about the words in parentheses ( ). Then write a short answer.

EXAMPLES Workers pay tax. (lottery winners) (yes)

Do lottery winners pay tax? Yes, they do.

Washington, D.C., is on the east coast. (New York) (yes)

Is New York on the east coast? Yes, it is.

1. Sara works from Monday to Friday. (on the weekend) (no)

_____

2. You are interested in American culture. (the American government) (yes)

_____

3. The president lives in the White House. (the vice president) (no)

_____

4. The museums are free. (the metro) (no)

_____

5. Washington has a space museum. (a zoo) (yes)

_____

6. Taxes are necessary. (popular) (no)

_____

7. Security is high in government offices. (in airports) (yes)

_____

8. People hate the IRS. (you) (yes)

_____

9. The metro runs all day. (after midnight) (no)

_____

10. The metro in Washington is clean. (quiet) (yes)

_____

Washington, D.C. Subway Map

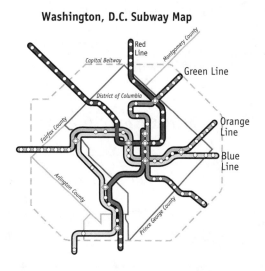

2.10 | *Or* Questions

Examples	Explanation
Do you study English **or** French? I study English.	An *or* question gives a choice of answers.
Is Washington, D.C., on the east coast **or** the west coast? It's on the east coast.	
Pronunciation Note: The first part of an *or* question has rising intonation; the second part has falling intonation. Listen to your teacher pronounce the examples above.	

EXERCISE **21**   ABOUT YOU Circle the words that are true for you, and make a statement about yourself. Then ask an *or* question. Another student will answer.

EXAMPLE   I drink (coffee) / *tea* in the morning. *I drink coffee in the morning*

A: Do you drink coffee or tea in the morning?
B: I drink coffee, too.

1. I speak *English / my native language* at home.

_____

2. I prefer *classical music / popular music.*

_____

3. I'm *a resident of the U.S. / a visitor.*

_____

4. I'm *married / single.*

_____

5. I live in *a house / an apartment / a dormitory.*

_____

6. I write with my *right hand / left hand.*

_____

7. I'm from *a big city / a small town.*

_____

8. I prefer *morning classes / evening classes.*

_____

9. I prefer to *eat out / eat at home.*

_____

10. English is *easy / hard* for me.

_____

11. I live *with someone / alone.*

_____

2.11 | *Wh-* Questions with the Simple Present Tense

Examples					Explanation
Wh-	*Does*	Subject	Verb	Complement	To form a question with *he, she, it, everyone, family,* or a singular subject, use:
Where	**does**	Barbara	**work?**		
When	**does**	she	**use**	the metro?	*Wh-* word + *does* + subject + base form
How	**does**	the IRS	**use**	your money?	Use the base form after *do* or *does.*
					Wrong: Where does Barbara *works?*
Wh-	*Do*	Subject	Verb	Complement	To form a question with *I, you, we, they,* and plural subjects, use:
When	**do**	we	**pay**	taxes?	
Where	**do**	they	**work?**		*Wh-* word + *do* + subject + base form
Why	**do**	I	**get**	a refund?	
Wh- Word	*Do/ Does*	Subject	Verb	Preposition	In informal written and spoken English, we usually put the preposition at the end of a *wh-* question.
Where	do	you	come	**from?**	
Who	does	she	live	**with?**	
What floor	do	you	live	**on?**	
Preposition	*Wh-*	*Do*	Subject	Verb	In formal written and spoken English, we put the preposition before the question word.
With	whom	do	you	live?	
On	what floor	do	you	live?	

Language Note:
We use *whom,* not *who,* after a preposition. We often use *who* when the preposition is at the end of the sentence. Compare:

Formal: With whom do you study?
Informal: Who do you study **with?**

EXERCISE 22 ABOUT YOU Answer the questions.

EXAMPLE   Where do you live?
I live near the school.

1. Who do you live with?
2. What do you bring to class?
3. What does the teacher bring to class?
4. What do you do after class?
5. How do you come to school?
6. Where do you live?
7. What do you like to do on weekends?
8. Why does the teacher give homework?

2.12 | Comparing Statements and Questions in the Simple Present Tense

Affirmative Statements and Questions

Wh- Word	Do/Does	Subject	Verb	Complement	Short Answer
		My sister	works	in Washington.	
	Does	she	work	for the IRS?	No, she doesn't.
Where	does	she	work?		
		You	pay	tax.	
	Do	you	pay	income tax?	Yes, I do.
Why	do	you	pay	tax?	

Negative Statements and Questions

Wh- Word	Don't/Doesn't	Subject	Verb	Complement
		People	don't like	taxes.
Why	don't	they	like	taxes?
		Sara	doesn't get	a tax refund.
Why	doesn't	she	get	a tax refund?

EXERCISE 23 ABOUT YOU Ask and answer questions with the words given. First ask a *yes/no* question. Then use the words in parentheses ( ) to ask a *wh-* question, if possible.

EXAMPLES   live near school (where)   have cable TV (why)

A: Do you live near school?   A: Do you have cable TV?
B: Yes, I do.   B: No, I don't.
A: Where do you live?   A: Why don't you have cable?
B: I live on Green and Main.   B: Because it's too expensive.

1. speak Spanish (what language)

2. have American friends (how many)

3. live near the school (where)

4. plan to go back to your country (when) (why)

5. live alone (with whom OR who . . . with)

6. practice English outside of class (with whom OR who . . . with)

7. bring your dictionary to class (why)

8. have a cell phone (why)

EXERCISE 24 First ask the teacher a *yes/no* question. After you get the answer, use the words in parentheses ( ) to ask a *wh-* question, if possible. Your teacher will answer.

EXAMPLE teach summer school (why)
A: Do you teach summer school?
B: No, I don't.
A: Why don't you teach summer school?
B: Because I like to travel in the summer.

1. have a laptop computer (what kind of computer)

2. speak another language (what language)

3. teach summer school (why)

4. correct the homework in school (where)

5. drive to school (how . . . get to[4] school)

6. like to teach English (why)

7. come from this city (what city . . . from)

EXERCISE 25 Ask and answer questions about another teacher with the words given. First ask a *yes/no* question. Then use the words in parentheses ( ) to ask a *wh-* question, if possible.

EXAMPLE speak your language (what languages)
A: Does your teacher speak your language?
B: No, he doesn't.
A: What languages does he speak?
B: He speaks English and French.

1. give a lot of homework (why)

2. write on the chalkboard (when)

3. come to class late (what time)

4. pronounce your name correctly (how)

5. use a textbook (what textbook)

6. wear jeans to class (what)

[4]*Get to* means arrive at.

2.13 | Questions About Meaning, Spelling, and Cost

Wh- Word	*Do/Does*	Subject	*Verb*	Complement	Explanation
What	does	"D.C."	mean?		*Mean, spell, say,* and *cost* are verbs and should be in the verb position of a question.
How	do	you	spell	"government"?	
How	do	you	say	"government" in your language?	
How much	does	a metro ticket	cost?		

EXERCISE 26 Fill in the blanks in the conversation below with the missing words.

A: What _____'s_____ your name?
  (example)

B: My name is Martha Gomez.

A: How _____ spell "Gomez"?
  (1)

B: G-O-M-E-Z. It's a Spanish name.

A: Are you _____ Spain?
  (2)

B: No, I'm _____.
  (3)

A: What country _____ you come _____?
  (4)   *(5)*

B: I come from Guatemala.

A: What language _____ they _____ in Guatemala?
  (6)   *(7)*

B: They speak Spanish in Guatemala.

A: _____ your family here?
  (8)

B: No. My family is still in Guatemala. I call them once a week.
A: Isn't that expensive?

B: No, it _____. I use a phone card.
  (9)

A: How much _____ cost?
  (10)

B: It _____ five dollars. We can talk for 35 minutes. I like
  (11)

  to say hello to my family every week.

A: How _____ "hello" in Spanish?
  (12)

B: We say "hola." Please excuse me now. I'm late for my class. *Hasta luego.*

A: What _____ "hasta luego" _____?
    (12)   *(13)*

B: It means "see you later" in Spanish.

2.14 | Comparing *Wh-* Questions—*Be* and Other Verbs

Examples	Explanation
Who **is** she? Where **does** she **live**? How **are** you? How **do** you **feel**? Where **am** I? What **do** I **need**?	Don't forget to use *do* or *does* in a question with a simple present-tense verb. *Wrong: Where she lives?* *Wrong: How you feel?* Don't use *be* to form a simple present-tense question. *Wrong: What am I need?*

EXERCISE 27 Read this conversation between two new students, Ricardo (R) and Alexander (A). Fill in the blanks with the missing words.

R: Hi. My name _____ 's _____ Ricardo.
              (example)

   What _____?
                    (1)

A: Alexander.

R: Nice to meet you, Alexander. Where _____?
                                                  (2)

A: I _____ from Ukraine.
                  (3)

R: What languages _____?
                          (4)

A: I speak Ukrainian and Russian.

R: _____ a new student?
                  (5)

A: Yes, I am. What about you? Where _____ from?
                                            (6)

R: I _____ from Peru.
              (7)

A: Where _____?
(8)

R: It's in South America. We speak Spanish in Peru. I want to learn English and then go back to my country.

A: Why _____ to go back to Peru?
(9)

R: Because my father has an export business there, and I want to work with him.

A: What _____?
(10)

R: "Export" means to sell your products in another country.

A: Why _____ to know English?
(11)

R: I need to know English because we have many American customers.

A: How many languages _____?
(12)

R: My father speaks four languages: English, French, German, and Spanish.

A: Tell me about your English class. _____ your
English teacher?   *(13)*

R: Oh, yes. I like her very much.

A: Who _____ your English teacher?
(14)

R: Barbara Nowak.

A: _____?
(15)

R: N-O-W-A-K. It's a Polish name.

A: How many students _____?
(16)

R: It has about 35 students. The classroom is very big.

A: What floor _____?
(17)

R: It's on the second floor.

A: When _____ your class _____?
(18)   *(19)*

R: It begins at 6 o'clock. I'm late. See you later.

A: _____ "see you later" in Spanish?
(20)

R: We say "hasta luego."

1. The simple present tense has two forms: the base form and the -s form:

Base Form		-s Form	
I		Everyone	
You		He	
We	eat.	She	eats.
They		It	
(Plural noun)		(Singular noun)	

2. Simple present-tense patterns with the -s form:

AFFIRMATIVE:	The president **lives** in Washington, D.C.
NEGATIVE:	He **doesn't live** in New York.
YES/NO QUESTION:	**Does** he **live** in the White House?
SHORT ANSWER:	Yes, he **does.**
WH- QUESTION:	Where **does** the vice president **live?**
NEGATIVE QUESTION:	Why **doesn't** the vice president **live** in the White House?

3. Simple present-tense patterns with the base form:

AFFIRMATIVE:	We **study** English in class.
NEGATIVE:	We **don't study** American history in class.
YES/NO QUESTION:	**Do** we **study** grammar?
SHORT ANSWER:	Yes, we **do.**
WH- QUESTION:	Why **do** we **study** grammar?
NEGATIVE QUESTION:	Why **don't** we **study** history?

4. Present-tense patterns with the verb be:

AFFIRMATIVE:	The teacher **is** absent.
NEGATIVE:	She **isn't** here today.
YES/NO QUESTION:	**Is** she sick?
SHORT ANSWER:	No, she **isn't.**
WH- QUESTION:	Where **is** she?
NEGATIVE QUESTION:	Why **isn't** she here?

5. We use the simple present tense with:

General truths and facts	Washington, D.C., **has** over half a million people. Americans **speak** English.
Customs	Japanese people **take** off their shoes when they enter a house. Americans **don't visit** friends without an invitation.
Regular activities (More on this use in Lesson 3)	He **visits** his parents every summer. I **play** soccer once a week.

1. Don't forget to use the -s form when the subject is *he, she, it,* or a singular noun.

   s
   He need more money.
        ^

   has
   This school ~~have~~ a big library.

2. Use the base form after *does* and *doesn't.*

   have
   My father doesn't ~~has~~ a car.

   Does your mother speaks English well?

3. If you are living in the U.S., use the American form, not the British form, with *have.*

   doesn't have
   He ~~hasn't~~ a car.

   Do you have
   ~~Have you~~ a car?

4. Don't forget *do/does* in a question.

   do
   Where your parents live?
        ^

5. Use correct word order in a question.

   your brother live
   Where does ~~live your brother~~?

   does your father have
   What kind of car ~~has your father~~?

   don't you
   Why ~~you don't~~ like pizza?

6. Don't use *be* with another verb to form the simple present tense.

   I
   ~~I'm~~ have three brothers.
   She's lives in New York.

   I don't
   ~~I'm not~~ have a car.

7. Don't use *be* in a simple present-tense question that uses another verb.

   Does
   ~~Is~~ your college have a computer lab?

   Do
   ~~Are~~ you speak French?

8. Use correct spelling for the -*s* form.

studies
She ~~studys~~ in the library.

watches
He ~~watchs~~ TV every evening.

9. Use the correct negative form.

doesn't
He ~~not~~ know the answer.

don't
They ~~no~~ speak English.

10. Don't use an -*ing* form for simple present tense.

write
I ~~writing~~ a letter to my family once a week.

11. *Family* is a singular word. Use the -*s* form.

s
My family live in Germany.

12. Use the same auxiliary verb in a short answer as in a *yes/no* question.

am
Are you hungry? Yes, I ~~do~~.

do
Do you like baseball? Yes, I ~~am~~.

13. Use the correct word order with questions about meaning, spelling, and cost.

does "wonderful" mean
What ~~means "wonderful"~~?

do bananas cost
How much ~~cost bananas~~ this week?

do you
How spell "opportunity"?

do you
How say "opportunity" in your language?

PART 1 Find the mistakes with the underlined words and correct them. Not every sentence has a mistake. If the sentence is correct, write *C*.

EXAMPLES ~~I'm not~~ *I don't* speak English well.

What <u>does</u> the teacher <u>want</u>? *C*

1. My mother <u>washes</u> my clothes every Sunday.

2. I <u>haven't</u> a dictionary.

3. <u>Where you</u> live?

4. He <u>no need</u> help from you.

5. My sister <u>talks</u> a lot.

6. You <u>aren't need</u> a dictionary for the test.

7. My brother <u>goes</u> to a state university.

8. <u>Are</u> you want to buy a new computer?

9. <u>Does</u> your apartment <u>have</u> a dishwasher? Yes, it <u>is</u>.

10. What kind of computers <u>has this school</u>?

11. <u>How spell</u> "computer"?

12. What <u>does the teacher want</u>?

13. Why <u>you don't</u> want to practice English at home?

14. How many children <u>do</u> your sister <u>have</u>?

15. How much <u>costs a stamp</u>?

16. The teacher <u>doesn't speak</u> my language.

17. My mother <u>worries</u> a lot about me.

18. Miami <u>don't have</u> cold winters.

19. I'm <u>not like</u> to use public transportation.

20. <u>How say</u> "potato" in your language?

21. My friend <u>going</u> to Puerto Rico every winter.

22. My family <u>has</u> a big house.

23. How many states <u>does the U.S. have</u>?

24. What <u>means</u> "adjective"?

PART 2 Write the -s form of the following verbs. Use correct spelling.

EXAMPLE take_____*takes*_____

1. go _____

2. carry _____

3. mix _____

4. drink _____

5. play _____

6. study _____

7. catch _____

8. say _____

PART 3 Fill in the first blank with the affirmative form of the verb in parentheses ( ). Then write the negative form of this verb.

EXAMPLES A monkey ____*lives*____ in a warm climate.
(live)

It _*doesn't live*_ in a cold climate.

Brazil ____*is*____ a big country.
(be)

Haiti ____*isn't*____ a big country.

1. The English language _____ the Roman alphabet.
(use)

The Chinese language _____ the Roman alphabet.

2. We _____ English in class.
(speak)

We _____ our native languages in class.

3. March _____ 31 days.
(have)

February _____ 31 days.

4. Mexico and Canada _____ in North America.
(be)

Colombia and Ecuador _____ in North America.

5. You _____ the "k" in "bank."
(pronounce)

You _____ the "k" in "knife."

6. The teacher _____ the English language.
(teach)

He/She _____ American history.

7. A green light _____ "go."
(mean)

A yellow light _____ "go."

8. I _____ from another country.
(come)

I _____ from the U.S.

9. English _____ hard for me.
(be)

My language _____ hard for me.

PART **4** Write a *yes/no* question about the words in parentheses ( ).
Then write a short answer.

EXAMPLES　January has 31 days. (February) (no)
Does February have 31 days? No, it doesn't.

China is in Asia. (Korea) (yes)
Is Korea in Asia? Yes, it is.

1. The U.S. has 50 states. (Mexico) (no)

_____

2. The post office sells stamps. (the bank) (no)

_____

3. San Francisco is in California. (Los Angeles) (yes)

_____

4. The metro runs all day. (all night) (no)

_____

5. January and March have 31 days. (April and June) (no)

_____

6. The president lives in the White House. (the vice president) (no)

_____

7. Americans speak English. (Canadians) (yes)

_____

8. We come to class on time. (the teacher) (yes)

_____

9. The museums have good security. (the White House) (yes)

_____

PART 5 Read each statement. Then write a _wh-_ question about the words in parentheses ( ). You don't need to answer the question.

EXAMPLES February has 28 days. (March)
How many days does March have?

Mexico is in North America. (Venezuela)
Where is Venezuela?

1. Mexicans speak Spanish. (Canadians)

_____

2. The U.S. has 50 states. (Mexico)

_____

3. The president lives in the White House. (the vice president)

_____

4. Thanksgiving is in November. (Christmas)

_____

5. You spell "occasion" O-C-C-A-S-I-O-N: ("tomorrow")

_____

6. "Occupation" means job or profession. ("occasion")

_____

7. The president doesn't make the laws. (why)

_____

8. Marek comes from Poland. (you)

_____

PART 6 Read this interview. Fill in the blanks with the missing word.

A: How old _____are you_____?
(example)

B: I'm 30 years old.

A: _____ married?
(1)

B: No I'm single.

A: _____ with your parents?
(2)

B: No, I don't live with my parents.

A: Why _____ with your parents?
(3)

B: I don't live with my parents because they live in another city.

A: Where _____?
(4)

B: They live in Chicago.

A: _____ you _____ Washington?
(5)   (6)

B: Yes, I like it very much.

A: Why _____ Washington?
(7)

B: I like it because it has so many interesting museums and galleries. But I don't have time to visit these places very often. I work every day. When my parents visit, we go to galleries and museums.

A: When _____?
(8)

B: They visit me in the spring. They love Washington.

A: Why _____ Washington?
(9)

B: They love it because it's a beautiful, interesting city. And they love it because I'm here.

A: What kind of job _____?
(10)

B: I have a job with the government. I work in the Department of Commerce.

A: What _____?
(11)

B: Commerce means "business."

A: How _____?
(12)

B: C-O-M-M-E-R-C-E.

A: _____ your job?
(13)

B: Yes, I like my job very much.

A: _____?
(14)

B: I live a few blocks from the White House.

A: _____ have a car?
(15)

B: No, I don't. I don't need a car.

A: How _____ to work?
(16)

B: I go to work by metro. If I'm late, I take a taxi.

A: How much _____?
(17)

B: A taxi ride from my house to work costs about $12.

A: _____ clean?
(18)

B: Oh, yes. The metro is very clean.

A: _____ all night?
(19)

B: No, the trains don't run all night. They run until midnight.

A: In my city, we don't say "metro." We use a different word.

B: How _____ "metro" in your city?
(20)

A: We say "subway."

EXPANSION ACTIVITIES

Classroom Activities

1. Check (✓) all the items below that are true of you. Find a partner and compare your list to your partner's list. Write three sentences telling about differences between you and your partner. (You may read your list to the class.)

   a. ____ I have a cell phone.   g. ____ I play a musical instrument.

   b. ____ I own a home.   h. ____ I sing well.

   c. ____ I live in an apartment.   i. ____ I'm a good driver.

   d. ____ I exercise regularly.   j. ____ I like pizza.

   e. ____ I'm a vegetarian.   k. ____ I use an electronic calendar.

   f. ____ I live with my parents.   l. ____ I write with my left hand.

2. **Game:** One student thinks of the name of a famous person and writes this person's initials on the chalkboard. Other students ask questions to try to guess the name of this person.

SAMPLE QUESTIONS

Is he an athlete?   Is he tall?
Where does he come from?   How old is he?

3. **Game:** One student comes to the front of the room. He or she thinks of an animal and writes the name of this animal on a piece of paper. The other students try to guess which animal it is by asking questions. The person who guesses the animal is the next to come to the front of the room.

EXAMPLE

lion
Does this animal fly? No, it doesn't.
Does it live in water? No, it doesn't.
What does it eat? It eats meat.
Does this animal live in Africa? Yes, it does.

4. In a small group, discuss differences between classes and teachers in this school and another school you know.

EXAMPLES

In my college back home, students stand up when they speak. This class has some older people. In my native country, only young people study at college.

Write About it

Write about a tourist attraction in your country (or in another country you know something about).

Outside Activities

Interview an American about his or her favorite tourist place in the U.S. Why does he or she like this place? What does this place have?

Internet Activities

1. Using the Internet, find information about one of the following places: Disneyland, the White House, the Holocaust Museum, Ellis Island, Epcot Center, the Alamo, or any other American tourist attraction that interests you. Then answer these questions:

What is it?   What does it cost to enter?
Where is it?   What does it have?

2. Using the Internet, find information about a museum or place of special interest in this city. Then answer these questions:

What is it?   What does it cost to enter?
Where is it?   What does it have?

Additional Activities at **http://elt.thomson.com/gic**

GRAMMAR

Frequency Words with the Simple Present Tense
Prepositions of Time

CONTEXT: American Holidays

Three Special Days
The Fourth of July

Before You Read

1. What is your favorite holiday? When is it?
2. Do you celebrate Mother's Day? When?
3. Do you send cards for special occasions?

Read the following article. Pay special attention to the frequency words.

Did You Know?

Valentine's Day began in ancient Rome to honor Juno, the Roman goddess of women and marriage.

Valentine's Day is a day of love. It is **always** on February 14. On this day, people **often** give flowers or candy to their spouses or sweethearts. Candy manufacturers make candy or candy boxes in the shape of a heart. People **sometimes** send cards, called valentines, to close friends and relatives. Red is the color associated with Valentine's Day. A valentine **usually** has a red heart and a message of love. It **often** has a picture of Cupid, a symbol of romantic love. Florists sell a lot of red roses on Valentine's Day. Young children **usually** have a party at school and exchange cards.

Another special day is Saint Patrick's Day. It is **always** on March 17. It is really an Irish holiday, but many Americans like St. Patrick's Day even if they are not Irish. We **sometimes** say that on St. Patrick's Day everybody is Irish. In New York City, there is **always** a parade on St. Patrick's Day. Green is the color associated with St. Patrick's Day. People **often** wear green clothes on this day. One symbol of St. Patrick's Day is the shamrock.

Businesses are **never** closed for Valentine's Day or St. Patrick's Day. People **never** take a day off from work for these days. Schools and government offices are **always** open (except if these days fall on a Sunday).

Another special day is Mother's Day. It is **always** in May, but it isn't **always** on the same date. It is **always** on the second Sunday in May. People **usually** buy presents for their mothers and grandmothers or send special cards. Families **often** have dinner in a restaurant. Florists sell a lot of flowers on Mother's Day.

People enjoy these holidays. Greeting card companies also enjoy these holidays. They **always** sell a lot of cards and make a lot of money at these times.

3.1 | Frequency Words with the Simple Present Tense

Frequency Word	Frequency	Examples
Always	100%	Mother's Day is **always** in May.
Usually	↑	I **usually** take my mother out to dinner.
Often		People **often** wear green on St. Patrick's Day.
Sometimes		I **sometimes** watch the parade.
Rarely/Seldom	↓	We **rarely** give flowers to children.
Never	0%	Businesses are **never** closed for Valentine's Day.

EXERCISE 1 Choose the correct word to fill in the blanks.

EXAMPLE People _____*often*_____ give flowers or candy on Valentine's
          _(never, seldom, often)

Day.

1. Valentine's Day is _____ on February 14.
   (always, sometimes, never)

2. People _____ send valentine cards to their
   (rarely, often, never)

   sweethearts.

3. A valentine card _____ has a red heart and a
   (never, rarely, usually)

   message of love.

4. Young children _____ have a Valentine's Day party
   (usually, always, never)

   at school.

5. Saint Patrick's Day is _____ on March 17.
   (always, sometimes, never)

St. Patrick's Day Parade

6. A St. Patrick's Day card _____ has a red heart.
   (always, usually, never)

7. In New York City, there is _____ a parade on Saint
   (always, seldom, never)

   Patrick's Day.

8. Card companies _____ do a lot of business before
   (never, always, seldom)

   holidays.

9. Businesses are _____ closed for St. Patrick's Day
   (always, usually, never)

   and Valentine's Day.

10. Mother's Day is _____ in May.
   (always, usually, never)

11. Mother's Day is _____ on a Saturday in the U.S.
   (always, never, sometimes)

EXERCISE 2   Fill in the blank with an appropriate frequency word about this class or this school.

EXAMPLE   We *sometimes* use a dictionary in class.

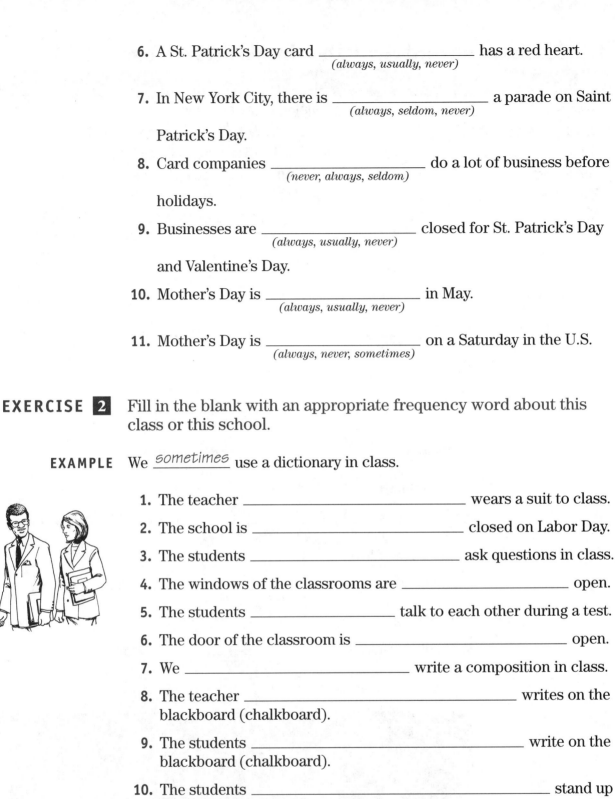

1. The teacher _____ wears a suit to class.

2. The school is _____ closed on Labor Day.

3. The students _____ ask questions in class.

4. The windows of the classrooms are _____ open.

5. The students _____ talk to each other during a test.

6. The door of the classroom is _____ open.

7. We _____ write a composition in class.

8. The teacher _____ writes on the
   blackboard (chalkboard).

9. The students _____ write on the
   blackboard (chalkboard).

10. The students _____ stand up
   when the teacher enters the room.

11. The teacher is _____ late to class.

12. We _____ read stories in class.

3.2 | Position of Frequency Words and Expressions

Examples	Explanation
Businesses *are* **never** closed for St. Patrick's Day. Mother's Day *is* **always** in May.	The frequency word comes after the verb *be*.
I **usually** *buy* a card for my mother. I **sometimes** *wear* green on St. Patrick's Day.	The frequency word comes before other verbs.
Sometimes I take my mother to a restaurant. **Usually** the weather is nice in May. **Often** we give gifts.	*Sometimes, usually,* and *often* can come at the beginning of the sentence, too.

EXERCISE 3 ABOUT YOU Add a frequency word to each sentence to make a **true** statement about yourself.

EXAMPLE   I eat fish.
I usually eat fish on Fridays.

1. I cook the meals in my house.

2. I stay home on Sundays.

3. I buy the Sunday newspaper.

4. I read the newspaper in English.

5. I use public transportation.

6. I'm tired in class.

7. I use my dictionary to check my spelling.

8. I buy greeting cards.

EXERCISE **4** Add a verb (phrase) to make a **true** statement about people from your country or cultural group.

EXAMPLE people / often

Russian people often go to the forest on the weekends to pick

mushrooms.

1. people / often

_____

2. people / seldom

_____

3. women / usually

_____

4. women / rarely

_____

5. men / usually

_____

6. men / rarely

_____

EXERCISE **5** ABOUT YOU Add a verb phrase to make a **true** statement about yourself.

EXAMPLE I / never

I never go to bed after 11 o'clock.

OR

I'm never in a good mood in the morning.

1. I / never

_____

2. I / always / in the morning

_____

3. I / usually / on Sunday

_____

4. I / often / on the weekend

_____

5. I / sometimes / in class

_____

EXERCISE 6 Use the words below to make sentences.

EXAMPLE mechanics / sometimes
Mechanics sometimes charge too much money.

1. American doctors / rarely

   _____

2. American teachers / sometimes

   _____

3. students at this school / often

   _____

4. this classroom / never

   _____

5. American hospitals / always

   _____

6. people in this country / often

   _____

THE FOURTH OF JULY

Before You Read

1. Do you like to see fireworks?
2. Do you celebrate any American holidays? What's your favorite American holiday?

 Read the following student composition. Pay special attention to prepositions of time.

My favorite holiday in the U.S. is American Independence Day. We celebrate it **on** July 4. In fact, we often call this holiday "The Fourth of July."

In the morning, my family and I prepare hamburgers for a barbecue. Our guests arrive **in** the afternoon, and we cook hamburgers and hotdogs on the grill in the backyard. We usually start to eat **at** about three o'clock. We have a lot of barbecues **in** the summer, but my favorite is **on** the Fourth of July.

We usually stay in our yard **from** about two o'clock **to** six o'clock p.m. Then **in** the evening, we usually go to the park. Most of our town goes there too, so we visit with each other while we wait for the fireworks. Finally, **at** night when it's completely dark, the fireworks show begins.

This is an exciting time for all of us. We celebrate our nation's independence and we have a lot of fun.

3.3 | Prepositions of Time

Preposition	Examples	Explanation
in	We prepare for the barbecue **in the morning.** We eat **in the afternoon.** We go to the park **in the evening.**	Use *in* with morning, afternoon, and evening.
in	Americans elect a president every four years: **in 2004, 2008, 2012,** etc.	Use *in* with years.
in	We often have a barbecue **in the summer.** It's too cold to have a barbecue **in the winter.**	Use *in* with seasons: summer, fall, winter, spring.
in	We celebrate Independence Day **in July.** We celebrate Mother's Day **in May.**	Use *in* with months.
on	We celebrate Independence Day **on July 4.** This year the holiday is **on Tuesday.**	Use *on* with dates and days.
at	We start to eat **at** three o'clock. We start the grill **at noon.** We go to bed **at midnight.**	Use *at* with a specific time of day.
at	The firework show starts **at night.**	Use *at* with night.
from . . . to	We stay in the backyard **from** two **to** six o'clock.	Use *from . . . to* with a beginning and an ending time. We can also say *from . . . till* or *until.*

EXERCISE 7 ABOUT YOU Answer these questions. Use the correct preposition.

1. What time do you get up in the morning?
2. What time do you go to bed at night?
3. What time does your English class begin?
4. What days does your English class meet?
5. What time do you get to school?
6. When do students have vacation?
7. When do you do your homework?
8. What hours do you go to school?
9. When is your birthday?

3.4 | Questions with *Ever*

We use *ever* in a question when we want an answer that has a frequency word.

Do/Does	Subject	*Ever*	Verb	Complement	Short Answer
Do	you	**ever**	cook	outside?	Yes, we **sometimes** do.
Does	your brother	**ever**	work	on a holiday?	Yes, he **often** does.

Be	Subject	*Ever*	Complement	Short Answer
Are	the stores	**ever**	open on a holiday?	Yes, they **sometimes** are.
Is	the park	**ever**	crowded on the Fourth of July?	Yes, it **always** is.

Language Notes:
1. In a short answer, the frequency word comes between the subject and the verb.
2. If the frequency word is *never,* don't use a negative verb.

    Is the school **ever** open on the Fourth of July?

        No, it **never** is.

    Do you **ever** buy fireworks?

        No, I **never** do.

EXERCISE 8 ABOUT YOU Add *ever* to ask these questions. Another student will answer.

EXAMPLES Do you eat in a restaurant?

A: Do you ever eat in a restaurant?
B: Yes, I often do. OR Yes, often.

Are you bored in class?

A: Are you ever bored in class?
B: No, I never am. OR No, never.

1. Do you use public transportation?
2. Do you drink coffee at night?
3. Do you drink tea in the morning?
4. Do you speak English at home?
5. Do you watch TV at night?
6. Do you rent DVDs?
7. Are you late to class?
8. Do you drive and use your cell phone at the same time?
9. Are you homesick?
10. Are you lazy on Saturdays?
11. Does it snow in March?
12. Do you ask for directions on the street?

EXERCISE 9 Add *ever* to these questions to ask about Americans. Another student will answer.

EXAMPLES Do Americans eat fast food?

A: Do Americans ever eat fast food?
B: Yes, they sometimes do.

Are Americans friendly to you?

A: Are Americans ever friendly to you?
B: Yes, they usually are.

1. Do Americans eat with chopsticks?
2. Do Americans carry radios?
3. Do Americans say, "Have a nice day"?
4. Do Americans kiss when they meet?
5. Do Americans pronounce your name incorrectly?
6. Are Americans impolite to you?
7. Do Americans shake hands when they meet?
8. Do Americans ask you what country you're from?
9. Are Americans curious about your native country?

EXERCISE 10 ABOUT YOU Fill in the blanks with a frequency word to make a statement about yourself. Then ask a question with *ever*. Another student will answer.

EXAMPLE I _____*never*_____ jog in the morning.

A: Do you ever jog in the morning?
B: No, I never do.

1. I _____ ride a bike in the summer.

2. I _____ visit relatives on Sunday.

3. I _____ go to sleep before 9 p.m.

    (Women: Do **A.** Men: Do **B.**)

4. **A.** I _____ wear high heels.

    B. I _____ wear a suit and tie.

5. I _____ do exercises.

6. I _____ eat meat.

7. I _____ drink colas.

8. I _____ buy the Sunday newspaper.

9. I _____ put sugar in my coffee.

10. I _____ take a nap in the afternoon.

11. I _____ eat in a restaurant.

12. I _____ use a fax machine.

13. I _____ bake bread.

14. I _____ use cologne or perfume.

15. I _____ take a bubble bath.

16. I _____ check my e-mail in the morning.

17. I _____ borrow money from a friend.

18. I _____ leave a light on when I sleep.

19. I _____ drink coffee at night.

20. I _____ listen to the radio when I'm driving.

3.5 | Questions with *How Often* and Answers with Frequency Expressions

We ask a question with *how often* when we want to know the frequency of an activity.

Examples	Explanation
How often do you eat hamburgers? 　Once in a while. **How often** do you visit your mother? 　Once a week. **How often** do you go to the park? 　Every week.	Expressions that show frequency are: • every day (week, month, year) • every other day (week, month, year) • from time to time • once in a while
I learn more about life in America **every day.** **Every day** I learn more about life in America. **From time to time,** I eat hamburgers. I eat hamburgers **from time to time.**	Frequency expressions can come at the beginning or the end of the sentence.

EXERCISE 11 ABOUT YOU Ask a question with "How often do you . . . ?" and the words given. Another student will answer.

EXAMPLE　get a haircut

　　A: How often do you get a haircut?
　　B: I get a haircut every other month.

1. come to class
2. shop for groceries
3. wash your clothes
4. use your cell phone
5. go out to dinner
6. use public transportation
7. renew your driver's license
8. buy the newspaper
9. go to the movies
10. check your e-mail

EXERCISE 12 Linda has a list to remind her of the things she has to do on a regular basis. Write questions and answers about her activities.

- drive daughter to ballet lessons—Tu, Th
- pick up son at baseball practice—Mon, Wed
- shop for groceries—Sat
- take the dog for a haircut—3rd day of every month
- go to the beauty salon—5th day of every month
- visit Mom—Fri
- go to the gym—Mon, Wed, Fri morning
- prepare the kids' lunches—Mon to Fri
- change oil in car—Jan, April, July, Oct

EXAMPLE *How often does she drive her daughter to ballet lessons?*

She drives her daughter to ballet lessons twice a week.

1. _____

_____

2. _____

_____

3. _____

_____

4. _____

_____

5. _____

_____

6. _____

_____

7. _____

_____

8. _____

_____

EXERCISE 13   ABOUT YOU Write a few sentences about a member of your family or another person you know. Use frequency words.

EXAMPLE   *My sister never helps with the housework.*

She sometimes leaves dirty dishes in the sink.

She always gets good grades.

_____

_____

EXERCISE 14   Use the words in parentheses ( ) to complete this conversation. Put the words in the correct order. Use the correct form of the verb.

A: Let's go to a movie tonight.

B: I can't. My mother _____*always makes*_____ dinner for me on Fridays.
(example: make/always)

If I don't visit her, she _____.
(1 complain/usually)

And if I don't call her, she worries.

A: _____ her?
(2 how/often/you/call)

B: _____.
(3 I/every day/call her)

A: Why do you call her so often?

B: She's old now, and she_____ lonely.
(4 often/be)

A: Well, invite your mother to go to the movies.

B: Thanks, but she has a favorite TV show on Friday nights.

She _____ it.
(5 watch/always)

A: _____ go out?
(6 ever/she)

B: She _____. She prefers to stay home.
(7 rarely/do)

She likes to cook, knit, and watch TV.

A: Is she a good cook?

B: Not really. She _____ the
(8 usually/cook)

same thing every week: chicken on Friday, fish on Saturday, meatloaf

on Sunday. . . . Her routine _____.
(9 change/never)

Only Mother's Day is different.

A: What _____ on Mother's Day?
(10 you/do/usually)

B: My sister and I _____ her flowers
(11 usually/buy)

and take her to a restaurant.

A: Does she like that?

B: Not really. She _____,
(12 usually/say)

"Don't waste your money. Flowers _____ in a day
(13 die/always)

or two. And my cooking is better than restaurant food."

A: _____ hard to please?
(14 be/she/always)

B: Yes, she is.

A: _____ satisfied?
(15 be/she/ever)

B: Not usually. She _____,
(16 always/say)

"I don't want Mother's Day once a year. I want it every day."

EXERCISE 15 *Combination Exercise.* Read a student's composition about the Fourth of July. Find the mistakes with the underlined words and correct them. Add a form of the verb *be* where necessary. If the underlined words are correct, write *C*.

My favorite holiday in the U.S. <u>is</u> the Fourth of July. My [*C*]

always puts
family <u>~~puts always~~</u> an American flag in front of the house.

My friends and relatives <u>always get</u> together for a BBQ.

We usually <u>cook</u> hamburgers and hotdogs on the grill.

<u>Sometimes we</u> cook fried chicken and steaks. The men in

the family usually <u>cooking</u>. (They <u>rarely cook</u> the rest of

the year!) We <u>usually have</u> the BBQ at my house, but

sometimes <u>we're have</u> the BBQ in a park. We always <u>has</u>

a potluck; everyone <u>brings</u> a different dish. My mother

always <u>bake</u> a delicious apple pie.

Our city always has a parade <u>at</u> the Fourth of July <u>from</u> noon <u>at</u> one o'clock. <u>In the</u> night, we usually go to see the fireworks at the main park. The park <u>always is</u> crowded. The weather usually nice, but <u>it's</u> sometimes rains and the fireworks show is canceled. When that <u>happen</u>, we are very disappointed. Luckily, that <u>seldom happens</u>.

Most businesses and schools <u>is</u> closed on the Fourth of July. The library, banks, and offices <u>are always</u> closed. <u>I'm</u> never work on this holiday, but my brother is a police officer and he sometimes <u>work</u> on the Fourth of July. Some businesses, such as supermarkets, <u>stays</u> open for half the day. People often <u>forgets</u> to buy something and need to get some last minute items.

I always look forward to this holiday because I <u>see</u> all my family and we <u>has</u> a lot of fun together. Also my birthday is <u>on</u> July and I get a lot of presents.

SUMMARY OF LESSON 3

1. Frequency Words:

Most Frequent	always	100%
↑	usually	↑
	often	
	sometimes	
↓	rarely/seldom	↓
Least Frequent	never	0%

2. The Position of Frequency Words:

AFTER THE VERB *BE*: He is **always** late.

BEFORE A MAIN VERB: I **usually** walk to work.

3. The Position of Frequency Expressions:
   Every day I watch TV.
   I watch TV **every day.**

4. Frequency Questions and Answers:
   Do you **ever** wear a suit? I seldom do.
   Are you **ever** bored in class? Yes, sometimes.
   How often do you go to the library? About once a month.

5. Review prepositions of time on page 84. Review the simple present tense in Lessons 1 and 2.

EDITING ADVICE

1. Put the frequency word in the correct place.

   am never
   I ~~never am~~ bored in class.

   I always
   ~~Always I~~ drink coffee in the morning.

2. Don't separate the subject and the verb with a frequency phrase.

   once in a while
   She ~~once in a while~~ visits her grandmother ⌃.

   Every other day we
   ~~We every other day~~ write a composition.

3. Don't use a negative verb with *never*.

   do
   Do you ever take the bus to school? No, I never ~~don't~~.
   We never ~~don't~~ eat in class.

4. Use *ever* in questions. Answer the question with a frequency word.

   sometimes
   Do you ever listen to the radio in the morning? Yes, I ~~ever~~ do.

LESSON 3 TEST/REVIEW

PART 1 Find the mistakes with the underlined words and correct them (including mistakes with word order). Not every sentence has a mistake. If the sentence is correct, write *C*.

EXAMPLES Do you ever drink coffee? No, I never ~~don't~~. *do*
I never eat spaghetti. *C*

1. <u>Always I</u> give my mother a present for Mother's Day.

2. I <u>rarely go</u> downtown.

3. <u>They never are</u> on time.

4. <u>It snows seldom</u> in April.

5. Do you ever take the bus? <u>Yes, I never do.</u>

6. <u>Are you ever</u> late to class? Yes, <u>always I am.</u>

7. Do you ever use chopsticks? Yes, <u>I ever do.</u>

8. <u>What often</u> do you go to the library? I go to the library <u>twice a month.</u>

9. I <u>once in a while</u> eat in a restaurant.

10. <u>Every other day</u> she cooks chicken.

PART 2   This is a conversation between two students. Fill in the blanks to complete the conversation.

A: Who _____*is*_____ your English teacher?
                (example)

B: His name _____ David.
                  (1)

A: _____ David?
                 (2)

B: Yes. I like him very much.

A: _____ he wear a suit to class?
        (3)

B: No, he _____. He always _____
        (4)   *(5)*

    jeans and running shoes.

A: _____?
                 (6)

B: He _____ about 60 years old.
        (7)

A: _____ your language?
                 (8)

B: No, he doesn't speak Spanish, but he _____ Polish
                                 (9)

    and Russian. And English, of course.

A: _____ does your class meet?
        (10)

B: It meets three days a week: Monday, Wednesday, and Friday.

A: My class _____ two days a week: Tuesday and
                     (11)

Thursday.

B: Tell me about your English teacher.

A: Her name _____ Dr. Misko. She never
                     (12)

_____ jeans to class. She _____
        (13)   (14)

wears a dress or suit. She _____ my language.
                                               (15)

She only _____ English.
                     (16)

B: Do you like her?

A: Yes, but she _____ a lot of homework and tests.
                              (17)

B: _____ does she give a test?
              (18)

A: Once a week. She gives a test every Friday. I _____
                                                                              (19)

like tests.

B: My teacher sometimes teaches us American songs.

_____ your teacher _____
        (20)   (21)

_____ you American songs?
        (22)

A: No, she never _____.
                              (23)

B: What book _____?
                          (24)

A: My class uses *Grammar in Context*.

B: What _____?
                     (25)

A: "Context" means the words that help you understand a new word or
idea.

B: How _____?
                   (26)

A: C-O-N-T-E-X-T.

PART **3** Fill in the blanks with the correct preposition.

EXAMPLE Many people go to church ____*on*____ Sundays.

1. We have classes _____ the evening.

2. Valentine's Day is _____ February.

3. Valentine's Day is _____ February 14.

4. A news program begins _____ 6 o'clock.

5. I watch TV _____ night.

6. We have vacation _____ the summer.

7. Many Americans work _____ 9 _____ 5 o'clock.

8. I drink coffee _____ the morning.

9. I study _____ the afternoon.

PART 4 Read this student's composition about his teacher. Find the mistakes with the underlined words, and correct them. Add the verb *be* where necessary. If the underlined words are correct, write *C*.

        is   *teaches*
      My English teacher ∧Barbara Nowak. She ~~teach~~ grammar and composition at City College. <u>She very</u> nice, but <u>she's</u> very strict. She <u>give</u> a lot of homework, and we <u>take</u> a lot of tests. If I pass the test, <u>I very</u> happy. <u>English's</u> hard for me.

      <u>Every day</u>, at the beginning of the class, she <u>takes</u> attendance and we <u>hand</u> in our homework. Then <u>she's explains</u> the grammar. We <u>do</u> exercises in the book. The book <u>have</u> a lot of exercises. Most exercises <u>is</u> easy, but some are hard. Sometimes we <u>says</u> the answers out loud, but sometimes we <u>write</u> the answers. Sometimes the teacher <u>asks</u> a student to write the answers on the chalkboard.

      The students <u>like</u> Barbara because she <u>make</u> the class interesting. She <u>brings often</u> songs to class, and we <u>learn</u> the words. Sometimes we <u>watch</u> a movie in class. <u>Always I</u> enjoy her lessons.

      After class I <u>sometimes going</u> to her office if I want more help. <u>She very</u> kind and always <u>try</u> to help me.

      Barbara <u>dresses</u> very informally. <u>Sometimes she wears</u> a skirt, but <u>she wears usually</u> jeans. <u>She about</u> 35 years old, but <u>she's looks</u> like a teenager. (In my country, <u>never a teacher wear</u> jeans.)

      <u>I very</u> happy with my teacher. She <u>understand</u> the problems of a foreigner because <u>she's</u> also a foreigner. <u>She's comes</u> from Poland, but she <u>speaks</u> English very well. She <u>know</u> it's hard to learn another language.

Classroom Activities

1. Find a partner. Interview your partner about one of his or her teachers, friends, or relatives. Ask about this person's usual activities.

   EXAMPLE
   A: What's your math teacher's name?
   B: Her name is Kathy Carlson.
   A: Does she give a lot of homework?
   B: No, she doesn't.
   A: What does she usually wear to class?
   B: She usually wears a skirt and blouse.
   A: Does she ever wear jeans to class?
   B: No, she never does.

2. In a small group or with the entire class, use frequency words to talk about the activities of a famous person (the president, a singer, an actor, etc.).

   EXAMPLE   The president of the U.S. often meets with leaders of other countries.

3. Find a partner. Talk about a special holiday that you and your family celebrate. Ask your partner questions about the date of the holiday, food, clothing, preparations, activities, and so on.

   EXAMPLE
   A: We celebrate the Lunar New Year.
   B: Do you wear special clothes?
   A: Yes, we do.
   B: What kind of clothes do you wear?

4. Look at the list of Linda's activities on page 89. Write a list to remind yourself of things you do on a regular basis. Find a partner. Compare your list to your partner's list.

5. Describe your favorite holiday to your classmates.

6. In the left column is a list of popular customs in the U.S. Do people in your native country or cultural group have similar customs? If so, put a check (✓) in Column A. If not, put a check (✓) in Column B. Discuss your answers in a group.

American Customs	A Similar custom in my native country or cultural group	B Completely different custom in my native country or cultural group
1. Americans often say, "Have a nice day."		
2. When someone sneezes, Americans usually say, "God bless you."		
3. Americans often ask, "How are you?" People usually reply, "I'm fine, thanks. How are you?"		
4. Americans rarely visit their friends without calling first.		
5. Americans are often in a hurry. They rarely have free time.		
6. Americans often eat popcorn in a movie theater.		
7. Americans often eat in fast-food restaurants.		
8. Americans often say, "OK."		
9. Americans often wear shorts and sandals in the summer.		
10. Americans often listen to a personal stereo.		
11. When eating, Americans usually hold a fork in the right hand and a knife in the left hand.		
12. Banks in the U.S. often have a time/temperature sign.		
13. American restaurants usually have salt and pepper shakers on the table.		
14. When a radio or TV breaks down, Americans often buy a new one. They rarely try to repair it.		
15. Americans often send greeting cards to close friends and relatives for birthdays, anniversaries, holidays, and illnesses.		
16. The Sunday newspaper often has store coupons.		
17. There is a special day for sweethearts, like Valentine's Day.		

Write About it

1. Write about one of your teachers. Describe your teacher and tell about his or her classroom behavior and activities.

2. Write about a holiday that you celebrate. Explain how you celebrate this holiday. Or write about how you celebrate your birthday or another special day.

Outside Activities

1. Ask an American-born person to do Exercise 4. See how your answers compare to this person's answers. Report this person's answers to the class.

2. Go to a drugstore, supermarket, or card store. Is there a special holiday at this time (for example, Father's Day, Thanksgiving, Christmas, Chanukah)? Read the messages in a few cards. Make a card for someone you know. Write your own message.

Internet Activities

1. Find a greeting card site on the Internet. Send an electronic greeting card to someone you know.

2. Using the Internet, find the answers to these questions:
   a. When is Father's Day in the U.S.?
   b. What is the origin of Mother's Day?
   c. When is Thanksgiving?
   d. What is the history of the Fourth of July?

Additional Activities at **http://elt.thomson.com/gic**

LESSON

4

GRAMMAR

Singular and Plural
Articles and Quantity Words
There + *Be* + Noun

CONTEXT: Americans and Where They Live

Americans and Where They Live
Finding an Apartment
Calling About an Apartment

101

4.1 | Singular and Plural—An Overview

Examples	Explanation
Some kids live with one **parent.** Some kids live with two **parents.** Everyone pays **taxes.**	Singular means one. Plural means more than one. Plural nouns usually end in -s or -es.
Some young **men** and **women** live with their parents. Some **children** live with their grandparents.	Some plural forms are irregular. They don't end in -s. **Examples:** man → men woman → women child → children

AMERICANS AND WHERE THEY LIVE[1]

Before You Read

1. Do you know anyone who lives alone?
2. Does your family own a house or rent an apartment?

Read the following information. Pay special attention to plural nouns.

There are about 295 million **people** in the U.S.

- The average family has 3.17 **people.**
- 5.5% of **children** live in **households** run by one or both **grandparents.**
- 69% of **children** live with two **parents.**
- 15% of **males** 25–34 live at home with one or both **parents.**
- 8% of **females** 25–34 live at home with one or both **parents.**
- 26% of **Americans** live alone. (Compare this to 8% in 1940.)
- 31% of **households** have a dog.
- 27% of **households** have a cat.

Homes
- 67% of American **families** own their **homes.**
- 25% of **homeowners** are over 65 **years** old.
- The price of **homes** depends on the city where you live. Some **cities** have very expensive **homes:** San Francisco, Boston, San Diego, Honolulu, and New York.
- The average American moves a lot. In a five-year period, 46% of **Americans** change their address. **Renters** move more than **owners.** Young **people** move more than older people.

[1] Statistics are from the 2000 census.

Average home prices in the most expensive American cities (2002)	
San Francisco	$541,000
Boston	$398,000
San Diego	$362,000
Honolulu	$330,000
New York City	$304,000

EXERCISE **1** Tell if the statement is true (T) or false (F).

EXAMPLE Homes in Boston are very expensive. **T**

1. Most children live with their grandparents.

2. Houses in New York City are more expensive than houses in San Francisco.

3. Most people rent an apartment.

4. Americans stay in the same house for most of their lives.

5. Cats are more popular than dogs in American homes.

6. Families in the U.S. are small (under five people).

7. Most children live with both parents.

8. The price of homes depends on where you live.

4.2 | Regular Noun Plurals

Word Ending	Example Words	Plural Addition	Plural form
Vowel	bee banana pie	+ s	bees bananas pies
Consonant	bed pin month	+ s	beds pins months
ss, sh, ch, x	class dish church box	+ es	classes dishes churches boxes
Vowel + y	boy day monkey	+ s	boys days monkeys
Consonant + y	lady story party	y + ies	ladies stories parties
Vowel + o	patio stereo radio	+ s	patios stereos radios
Consonant + o	mosquito tomato potato	+ es	mosquitoes tomatoes potatoes
Exceptions: photos, pianos, solos, altos, sopranos, autos, avocados.			
f or fe	leaf calf knife	f + ves fe + ves	leaves calves knives
Exceptions: beliefs, chiefs, roofs, chefs			

EXERCISE 2   Write the plural form of each noun.

EXAMPLES   leaf _____ *leaves* _____

toy _____ *toys* _____

1. dish _____   4. book _____

2. country _____   5. boy _____

3. half _____   6. girl _____

7. bench _____
8. box _____
9. shark _____
10. stereo _____
11. knife _____
12. story _____
13. sofa _____
14. key _____
15. movie _____
16. squirrel _____
17. mosquito _____
18. lion _____
19. fly _____

20. cow _____
21. table _____
22. roach _____
23. fox _____
24. house _____
25. turkey _____
26. chicken _____
27. wolf _____
28. dog _____
29. bath _____
30. pony _____
31. duck _____
32. moth _____

4.3 | Pronunciation of Plural Nouns

The plural ending has three pronunciations: /s/, /z/, and /əz/

Pronunciation	Rule	Examples
/s/	Pronounce /s/ after voiceless sounds: /p, t, k, f, θ/	lip—lips cat—cats rock—rocks cuff—cuffs month—months
/z/	Pronounce /z/ after voiced sounds: /b, d, g, v, m, n, ŋ, l, r/ and all vowels	cab—cabs can—cans lid—lids thing—things bag—bags bill—bills stove—stoves car—cars sum—sums bee—bees
/əz/	Pronounce /əz/ when the base form ends in *s, ss, ce, se, sh, ch, ge, x*	bus—buses class—classes place—places cause—causes dish—dishes beach—beaches garage—garages tax—taxes

EXERCISE 3 Go back to Exercise 2 and pronounce the plural form of each word.

4.4 | Irregular Noun Plurals

Singular	Plural	Explanation
man woman mouse tooth foot goose	men women mice teeth feet geese	Some nouns have a vowel change in the plural form. **Singular:** Do you see that old **woman?** **Plural:** Do you see those young **women?**
sheep fish deer	sheep fish deer	Some plural forms are the same as the singular form. **Singular:** I have one **fish** in my tank. **Plural:** She has ten **fish** in her tank.
child person mouse	children people (OR persons) mice	For some plurals we change to a different form. **Singular:** She has one **child.** **Plural:** They have two **children.**
	pajamas clothes pants/slacks (eye)glasses scissors	Some words have no singular form. **Example:** My **pants** are new. Do you like them?
dozen (12) hundred thousand million		Exact numbers use the singular form. **Examples:** The U.S. has over 290 **million** people. I need to buy **a dozen** eggs.
	dozens hundreds thousands millions	The plural form of a number is *not* an exact number. **Example:** **Thousands** of people live alone.

Language Notes:
1. You hear the difference between *woman* (singular) and *women* (plural) in the first syllable.
2. The plural of *person* can also be *persons*, but *people* is more common.

EXERCISE 4 The following nouns have an irregular plural form. Write the plural.

EXAMPLE   man ____men____

1. foot _____   5. fish _____

2. woman _____   6. mouse _____

3. policeman _____   7. sheep _____

4. child _____   8. tooth _____

EXERCISE 5 Fill in the blanks with the correct plural form of the noun in parentheses.

EXAMPLE   Some ___people___ like to live alone.
                      (person)

1. Most _____ in the U.S. own a house.
        (family)

2. The U.S. has over 290 million _____.
                                  (person)

3. Americans move many _____.
                        (time)

4. Most single _____ are _____.
               (parent)   *(woman)*

5. Some _____ earn more money than their _____.
        (woman)   *(husband)*

6. _____ are very expensive in some _____.
   (Home)   *(city)*

7. Divorce is very high in some _____.
                               (country)

   Some _____live with only one parent.
        (child)

8. How many square _____ does your house or apartment have?
                   (foot)

9. Some _____ live with _____.
        (child)   *(grandparent)*

10. The average family has 3.17 _____.
                                (person)

11. Some apartments have a problem with _____.
                                        (mouse)

Before You Read

1. Do you live in a house, an apartment, or a dorm?[2] Do you live alone?
2. Do you like the place where you live? Why or why not?

Read the following article. Pay special attention to *there + be* followed by singular and plural nouns.

There are several ways to find an apartment. One way is to look in the newspaper. **There is** an "Apartments for Rent" section in the back of the newspaper. **There are** many ads for apartments. **There are** also ads for houses for rent and houses for sale. Many newspapers also put their listings online.

Another way to find an apartment is by looking at the buildings in the neighborhood where you want to live. **There are** often "For Rent" signs on the front of the buildings. **There is** usually a phone number on the sign. You can call and ask for information about the apartment that you are interested in. You can ask:

- How much is the rent?
- Is heat included?
- What floor is the apartment on?
- **Is there** an elevator?
- How many bedrooms **are there** in the apartment?
- How many closets **are there** in the apartment?
- Is the apartment available[3] now?

If an apartment interests you, you can make an appointment to see it. When you go to see the apartment, you should ask some more questions, such as the following:

- **Is there a** lease?[4] How long is the lease?

---

[2] *Dorm* is short for *dormitory*, a building where students live.
[3] *Available* means ready to use now.
[4] A *lease* is a contract between the owner (landlord or landlady) and the renter (tenant). It tells how much the rent is, how long the tenant can stay in the apartment, and other rules.

- **Is there a** janitor or manager?
- **Is there a** parking space for each tenant? Is it free, or do I have to pay extra?
- **Are there** smoke detectors? (In many places, the law says that the landlord must put a smoke detector in each apartment and in the halls.)
- **Is there a** laundry room in the building? Where is it?

The landlord may ask you a few questions, such as:

- How many people **are there** in your family?
- Do you have any pets?

You should check over the apartment care-fully before you sign the lease. If **there are** some problems, you should talk to the landlord to see if he will take care of them before you move in.

4.5 | Using *There + Is/Are*

We use *there + is* or *there + are* to introduce a subject into the conversation when we show location or time.

	Examples				
Singular	*There*	*is*	*a/an/one*	**singular subject**	**location/time**
	There	is	a	janitor	in my building.
	There	is	an	open house	at 1:00.
	There	is	one	dryer	in the basement.
	There	is	a	rent increase	this year.
	Note: *There's* is the contraction for *there is*.				
Negative Singular	*There*	*isn't*	*a*	**singular subject**	**location/time**
	There	isn't	a	back door	in my apartment.
	There's	*no*		**singular subject**	**location/time**
	There's	no		balcony	in my apartment.
	There's	no		heat	this month.
Plural	*There*	*are*	**plural word**	**plural subject**	**location/time**
	There	are	several	windows	in the bedroom.
	There	are	many	children	in the building.
	There	are	some	cats	in the building.
	There	are	two	closets	in the hall.
	There	are	—	curtains	on the windows.
	Note: We don't write a contraction for *there are*.				
Negative Plural	*There*	*aren't*	**plural word**	**plural subject**	**location/time**
	There	aren't	any	shades	on the windows.
	There	aren't	any	new tenants	this month.
	There	*are*	*no*	**plural subject**	**location/time**
	There	are	no	cabinets	in the kitchen.

Language Notes:

1. When two nouns follow *there,* use a singular verb (*is*) if the first noun is singular. Use a plural verb (*are*) if the first noun is plural.

   There is a closet in the bedroom and two closets in the hall.

   There are two closets in the hall and one closet in the bedroom.

   There is a washer and dryer in the basement.

2. *There* never introduces a specific or unique noun. Don't use a noun with the definite article (*the*) after *there*.

   Wrong: *There's* the Eiffel Tower in Paris.

   Right: The Eiffel Tower is in Paris.

EXERCISE **6**   ABOUT YOU Use the words given to make a statement about the place where you live (house or apartment). If you live in a dorm, use Exercise 7 instead.

EXAMPLES   carpet / in the living room
There's a carpet in the living room.

trees / in front of the building
There are no trees in front of the building.

1. porch

2. blinds / on the windows

3. door / in every room

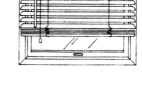

4. window / in every room

5. lease

6. closet / in the living room

7. number / on the door of the apartment

8. overhead light / in every room

9. microwave oven / in the kitchen

10. back door

11. fireplace

12. smoke detector

EXERCISE **7**   ABOUT YOU Make a statement about your dorm and dorm room with the words given. (If you live in an apartment or house, skip this exercise.)

EXAMPLES   window / in the room
There's a window in the room.

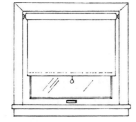

curtains / on the window
There are no curtains on the window
There are shades.

1. closet / in the room

2. two beds / in the room

3. private bath / for every room

4. men and women / in the dorm

5. cafeteria / in the dorm

6. snack machines / in the dorm

7. noisy students / in the dorm

8. numbers / on the doors of the rooms

9. elevator(s) / in the dorm

10. laundry room / in the dorm

4.6 | Questions and Short Answers Using *There*

Compare statements (S) and questions (Q) with *there*. Observe short answers (A).

	Examples	Explanation

Singular Statement
 	
Yes/No **Question**
	S: **There is** a laundry room in the building.
	
	Q: **Is there** an elevator in the building?
	A: Yes, there is.
	
	S: **There's** a closet in the bedroom.
	Q: **Is there** a closet in the hall?
	A: No, there isn't.
		Question word order:
		
		Is + *there* + *a/an* + singular noun . . . ?
		
		Short answers:
		   Yes, there is. (no contraction)
		   No, there isn't. OR No, there's not.

Plural Statement *Yes/No* **Question**	S: **There are** some children in the building. Q: **Are there** (any) children on your floor? A: Yes, there are. S: **There are** trees in back of the building. Q: **Are there** (any) trees in front of the building? A: No, there aren't.	**Question word order:** *Are* + *there* + *(any)* + plural noun . . . ? We often use *any* to introduce a plural noun in a *yes/no* question. **Short answers:** No, there aren't.
Plural Statement **Information Question**	S: **There are** ten apartments in my building. Q: **How many** apartments **are there** in your building? A: Thirty.	**Question word order:** *How many* + plural noun + *are there* . . . ?

EXERCISE 8 ABOUT YOU Ask and answer questions with *there* and the words given to find out about another student's apartment and building. (If you live in a dorm, use Exercise 9 instead.)

EXAMPLES a microwave oven / in your apartment

A: Is there a microwave oven in your apartment?
B: No, there isn't.

closets / in the bedroom

A: Are there any closets in the bedroom?
B: Yes. There's one closet in the bedroom.

1. children / in your building
2. a dishwasher / in the kitchen
3. a yard / in front of your building
4. trees / in front of your building
5. a basement / in the building
6. a laundry room / in the basement
7. a janitor / in the building
8. noisy neighbors / in the building
9. nosy[5] neighbors / in the building
10. an elevator / in the building
11. parking spaces / for the tenants
12. a lot of closets / in the apartment
13. how many apartments / in your building
14. how many parking spaces / in front of your building

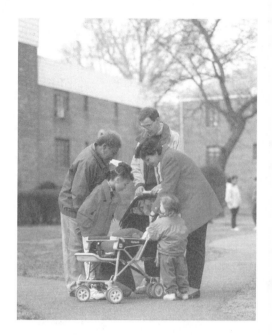

EXERCISE 9 ABOUT YOU Ask and answer questions with *there* and the words given to find out about another student's dorm. (If you live in an apartment or house, skip this exercise.)

EXAMPLE a bicycle room / in your dorm

A: Is there a bicycle room in your dorm?
B: No, there isn't.

1. married students
2. private rooms
3. a bicycle room
4. a computer room
5. an elevator
6. a bulletin board

7. graduate students
8. a quiet place to study
9. an air conditioner / in your room
10. a parking lot / for your dorm
11. how many rooms / in your dorm
12. how many floors / in your dorm

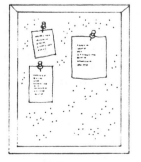

---

[5] A *nosy* person is a person who wants to know everyone's business.

EXERCISE 10 Use the words given to ask the teacher a question about his or her office. Your teacher will answer.

EXAMPLES pencil sharpener

A: Is there a pencil sharpener in your office?
B: No, there isn't.

books

A: Are there any books in your office?
B: Yes. There are a lot of books in my office.

1. phone
2. file cabinet
3. photos of your family
4. radio
5. copy machine
6. windows

7. calendar
8. bookshelves
9. plants
10. voice mail
11. fax machine
12. computer

EXERCISE 11 A student is calling about an apartment for rent. Fill in the blanks with *there is, there are, is there, are there,* and other related words to complete this phone conversation between the student (S) and the landlady (L).

S: I'm calling about an apartment for rent on Grover Street.

L: We have two apartments available. ___There's___ a four-room
   (example)
   apartment on the first floor and a three-room apartment on the fourth floor. Which one are you interested in?

S: I prefer the smaller apartment. _____ an elevator in the building?
   (1)

L: Yes, there is. How many people _____ in your family?
   (2)

S: It's just for me. I live alone. I'm a student. I need a quiet apartment. Is this a quiet building?

L: Oh, yes. _____ no kids in the building.
   (3)
   This is a very quiet building.

S: That's good. I have a car. _____ parking spaces?
   (4)

L: Yes. _____ 20 spaces in back of the building.
   (5)

S: How _____ apartments _____ in the building?
   (6)   (7)

L: _____ 30 apartments.
   (8)

S: Twenty parking spaces for 30 apartments? Then _____

_____ enough spaces for all the tenants.
   (9)

L: Don't worry. Not everyone has a car. Parking is on a first-come,

first-served basis.[6] And _____ plenty
                                    (10)

of[7] spaces on the street.

S: _____ a laundry room in the building?
       (11)

L: Yes. There are washers and dryers in the basement.

S: How much is the rent?

L: It's $850 a month.

S: I hear a dog. Is that your dog?

L: Yes, but don't worry. I don't live in the building. _____

no dogs in the building.   *(12)*

S: When can I see the apartment?

L: How about tomorrow at six o'clock?

S: That'll be fine. Thanks.

4.7 | *There* vs. *They* and Other Pronouns

Examples	Explanation
There's a *janitor* in the building. **He's** in the basement. **There's** a little *girl* in the next apartment. **She's** cute. **There's** an empty *apartment* on the first floor. **It's** available now. **There are** two washing *machines*. **They're** in the basement.	To introduce a new noun, we use *there* + *is/are*. When we use this noun again as the subject of another sentence, we use *he, she, it,* or *they*.

Pronunciation Note: We pronounce *there* and *they're* exactly the same. Listen to your teacher pronounce the sentences from the box above.

Spelling Note: Don't confuse *there* and *they're*.
   There are dogs in the next apartment.
   They're very friendly.

[6] A *first-come, first-served* basis means that people who arrive first will get something first (parking spaces, theater tickets, classes at registration).
[7] *Plenty of* means "a lot of."

EXERCISE 12   Fill in the blanks with *there's*, *there are*, *it's*, or *they're*.

EXAMPLE   ___There's___ a small apartment for rent in my building.

             ___It's___ on the fourth floor.

1. _____ two apartments for rent. _____ not on the same floor.

2. _____ a laundry room in the building. _____ in the basement.

3. The parking spaces are in the back of the building. _____ _____ for the tenants with cars.

4. The parking spaces don't cost extra. _____ free for the tenants.

5. The apartment is small. _____ on the fourth floor.

6. The building has 30 apartments. _____ a big building.

7. The student wants to see the apartment. _____ on Grover Street.

8. The building is quiet because _____ no kids in the building.

9. How much is the rent? _____ $850 a month.

10. Is the rent high? No, _____ not high.

11. _____ no dogs in the building.

12. _____ a quiet building.

EXERCISE 13   Ask a question about this school using *there* and the words given. Another student will answer. If the answer is "yes," ask a question with *where*.

EXAMPLE   lockers

A: Are there any lockers at this school?
B: Yes, there are.
A: Where are they?
B: They're near the gym.

1. a library
2. vending machines
3. public telephones
4. a computer room
5. a cafeteria
6. a gym
7. a swimming pool
8. tennis courts
9. dormitories
10. a parking lot
11. a bookstore
12. copy machines
13. a student lounge
14. a fax machine

CALLING ABOUT AN APARTMENT

Before You Read

1. Does your neighborhood have more apartment buildings or houses?

2. Do you prefer to live alone, with a roommate, or with your family? Why?

Read the following phone conversation between a student (S) and the manager (M) of a building. Pay special attention to the definite article (*the*), the indefinite articles (*a, an*), and indefinite quantity words (*some, any*).

S: Hello? I want to speak with **the landlord.**

M: I'm **the manager** of **the building.** Can I help you?

S: I need to find **a** new **apartment.**

M: Where do you live now?

S: I live in **a** big **apartment** on Wright Street. I have **a roommate,** but he's graduating, and I need **a** smaller **apartment.** Are there **any** small **apartments** for rent in your building?

M: There's one.

S: What floor is it on?

M: It's on **the** third **floor.**

S: Does it have **a bedroom?**

M: No. It's **a** studio **apartment.** It has **a living room** and **a kitchen.**

S: Is **the living room** big?

M: So-so.

S: Does **the kitchen** have **a stove** and **a refrigerator?**

M: Yes. **The refrigerator** is old, but it works well. **The stove** is pretty new.

S: Can I see **the apartment?**

M: I have a question for you first. Do you have **a dog?** We don't permit **dogs.** **Dogs** make a lot of noise.

S: I don't have **a dog.**

M: I'm happy to hear that.

S: But I have **a snake.**

M: **A snake?**

S: **Snakes** are quiet.

M: Yes, but . . .

S: Don't worry. I keep **the snake** in a glass box.

M: I hope **the box** is always closed.

S: It is. I only open it to feed **the snake.** I feed it **mice.**

M: Oh.

S: When can I see **the apartment?**

M: I have to speak to **the landlord.** I'm not sure if you can have **snakes** and **mice** in **the apartment.**

4.8 | Articles with Definite and Indefinite Nouns

Singular

Indefinite	Definite	Explanation
I live in **a** big building. There's **a** janitor in the building.	**The** building is near the college. **The** janitor lives on the first floor.	We introduce a singular noun with the indefinite articles (*a* or *an*). When we refer to this noun again, we use the definite article *the*.
	May I speak to **the** landlord? He lives on **the** third floor. **The** basement is dirty.	We use *the* before a singular noun if this noun is the only one or if the speaker and listener share an experience and are referring to the same one. (In this case, they are talking about the same building.)

Plural

Indefinite	Definite	Explanation
My building has **(some)** washing machines. Are there **(any)** dryers?	**The** washing machines are in the basement. Where are **the** dryers?	We introduce a plural noun with *some*, *any*, or no article. When we refer to this noun again, we use the definite article *the*.
	The tenants are angry. **The** washing machines don't work.	We use *the* before a plural noun if the speaker and the listener share the same experience. (In this case, they are talking about the same building.)

EXERCISE 14 Fill in the blanks in the conversations between two students. Use *the, a, an, some,* or *any.*

CONVERSATION 1

A: Is there _____*a*_____ cafeteria at this school?
         (example)

B: Yes, there is.

A: Where's _____ cafeteria?
                    (1)

B: It's on _____ first floor.
                 (2)

A: Are there _____ snack machines in _____ cafeteria?
                         (3)   *(4)*

B: Yes, there are.

A: I want to buy _____ soft drink.
                          (5)

B: _____ soft drink machine is out of order today.
         (6)

CONVERSATION 2

A: Is there _____ bookstore for this college?
(1)

B: Yes, there is.

A: Where's _____ bookstore?
(2)

B: It's on Green Street.

A: I need to buy _____ dictionary.
(3)

B: Today's _____ holiday. _____ bookstore is closed today.
(4)   (5)

EXERCISE 15 Fill in the blanks in the conversation about apartment problems. Use *the, a, an, some,* or *any.*

A: I have ____*a*____ problem in my apartment.
(example)

B: What's _____ problem?
(1)

A: _____ landlord doesn't provide enough heat. I have
(2)

to wear _____ sweater or _____ coat all the
(3)   (4)

time in the apartment.

B: Why don't you talk to _____ building manager?
(5)

Maybe _____ heating system is broken. If he doesn't
(6)

solve _____ problem, you can send _____
(7)   (8)

letter to _____ department of housing.
(9)

A: That's _____ good idea. There's one more problem.
(10)

I have _____ neighbor who has _____ small dog.
(11)   (12)

_____ dog barks all the time when _____ neighbor isn't
(13)   (14)

home. We share _____ wall, and I can hear _____ dog
(15)   (16)

barking through _____ wall.
(17)

B: Talk to _____ neighbor. Tell him there are dog services. For
(18)

_____ price, someone can go to his house every day and play
(19)

with _____ dog and take it out for a walk.
(20)

A: I don't think he wants to pay _____ price for this service.
(21)

B: Then talk to _____ landlord. Tell him about _____ problem.
(22)   (23)

4.9 | Making Generalizations

A generalization says that something is true of all members of a group.		
Singular	**Plural**	**Explanation**
A snake is quiet. **A dog** makes noise.	**Snakes** are quiet. **Dogs** make noise.	To make a generalization about the **subject,** use the indefinite article (*a* or *an*) with a singular subject or no article with a **plural** subject.
	I don't like **snakes.** Snakes eat **mice.**	To make a generalization about the **object,** use the plural form with no article.

EXERCISE **16**   The following sentences are generalizations. Change the subject from singular to plural. Make other necessary changes.

EXAMPLE: A single parent has a difficult life.
Single parents have a difficult life.

1. A house in San Diego is expensive.

   _____

2. A homeowner pays property tax.

   _____

3. A dog is part of the family.

   _____

4. A renter doesn't have freedom to make changes.

   _____

5. An owner has freedom to make changes.

   _____

EXERCISE 17 ABOUT YOU Use the noun in parentheses ( ) to give general information about your native country or hometown. Use the plural form with no article.

EXAMPLE (woman)
Generally, women don't work outside the home in my native country.

1. (person)   5. (house)
2. old (person)   6. poor (person)
3. (women)   7. (car)
4. (man)   8. (doctor)

EXERCISE 18 Add a plural subject to these sentences to make a generalization.

EXAMPLE _____*Small children*_____ need a lot of sleep.

1. _____ make a lot of money.
2. _____ have a hard life.
3. _____ talk on the phone a lot.
4. _____ are in good physical condition.
5. _____ believe in Santa Claus.
6. _____ worry about children.

EXERCISE 19 ABOUT YOU Use the plural form of each noun to tell if you like or don't like the following living conditions.

EXAMPLE tall building
I like tall buildings.

1. white wall   7. high ceiling
2. curtain on the window   8. bright light
3. picture on the wall   9. two-story house
4. plant   10. digital clock
5. friendly neighbor   11. carpet
6. blind on the window   12. hardwood floor

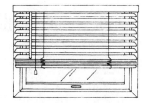

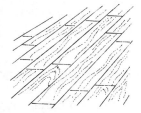

EXERCISE 20 ABOUT YOU Ask *Do you like* + the plural form of the noun. Another student will answer.

EXAMPLES child

A: Do you like children?
B: Yes, I do.

dog

A: Do you like dogs?
B: No, I don't.

1. cat
2. dog
3. American doctor
4. American car
5. American movie
6. fashion magazine

7. comic book
8. computer
9. computer game
10. strict teacher
11. American supermarket
12. American textbook

EXERCISE 21 Combination Exercise. This is a conversation between two students. Fill in the blanks with *the, a, an, some,* or *any*. Sometimes an article may not be necessary.

A: Is there _____*a*_____ copy machine in our library?
   (example)

B: Yes. There are several copy machines in _____ library.
   (1)

A: Are _____ copy machines free?
   (2)

B: No. You need to use _____ nickel[8] for
   (3)

   _____ copy machines. Why do you need
   (4)

   _____ copy machine?
   (5)

A: I want to copy my classmate's textbook.

B: The whole thing? Why?

A: _____ textbooks in the U.S. are too expensive.
   (6)

B: There's _____ rule about copying an entire book.
   (7)

A: What's _____ rule?
   (8)

B: You can't copy _____ books without permission
   (9)

   from the publisher.

[8] A *nickel* is a five-cent coin.

A: In my country, we copy _____ books all the time.
(10)

B: But it's illegal. People who copy _____ books,
(11)

CDs, and movies are called "pirates."

SUMMARY OF LESSON 4

1. Singular and Plural
    boy—boys
    box—boxes
    story—stories
    (Exceptions: men, women, people, children, feet, teeth)

2. *There + be*
    There's an empty apartment in my building.
    There are two washing machines in the basement.
    Are there any parking spaces?

3. Articles

    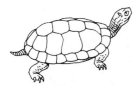

    * To make a generalization:
        SINGULAR   **A dog** has good hearing.
        PLURAL   **Dogs** have good hearing.
                I like **dogs.**

    * To introduce a new noun into the conversation:
        SINGULAR   I have **a dog.**
        PLURAL   I have **(some) turtles.**
                I don't have **(any) birds.**

    * To talk about a previously mentioned noun:
        SINGULAR   I have a dog. **The dog** barks when the letter
                carrier arrives.
        PLURAL   I have some turtles. I keep **the turtles** in the
                bathroom.

    * To talk about specific items or people from our experience:
        SINGULAR   **The janitor** cleans the basement once a week.
        PLURAL   **The tenants** have to take out their own garbage.

    * To talk about the only one:
        The president lives in Washington, D.C.
        The Statue of Liberty is in New York.

1. *People* is a plural noun. Use a plural verb form.

   are
   People in my country ~~is~~ very poor.

2. Don't use *the* with a generalization.

   _D_
   ~~The~~ dogs are friendly animals.

3. Don't confuse *there* with *they're*.

   They're
   I have two brothers. ~~There~~ in Florida.

4. Use *there + is/are* to introduce a new subject.

   there are
   In my class five students from Haiti.
       ^

5. Don't confuse *it's* and *there's*.

   There's
   ~~It's~~ a closet in my bedroom.

6. Don't confuse *have* and *there*.

   There's
   ~~Have~~ a closet in my bedroom.

7. Don't use *the* + a unique noun after *there*.

   _T_   _is_
   ~~There's~~ the Golden Gate Bridge in California.
                                      ^

8. Don't use *the* with the first mention of a noun when you and the listener do not share a common experience with this noun.

   _a_
   I have ~~the~~ new watch.

9. Don't use an apostrophe for a plural ending.

   brothers
   She has three ~~brother's~~.

PART **1** A woman is showing her new apartment to her friend. Find the mistakes with the underlined words in this conversation and correct them. If the sentence is correct, write *C*.

A: Let me show you around my new apartment.

B: <u>It's</u> a big apartment.   *C*

A: It's big enough for my family. ~~They're~~ *There* are four bedrooms and two bathrooms. <u>Has each bedroom a large closet.</u> Let me show you my
                   (1)
kitchen too.

B: Oh. <u>It's</u> a new dishwasher in your kitchen.
   (2)

A: <u>It's</u> wonderful. You know how I hate to wash dishes.
  (3)

B: <u>Is there</u> a microwave oven?
   (4)

A: No, <u>there isn't.</u>
    (5)

B: <u>Are any</u> washers and dryers for clothes?
   (6)

A: Oh, yes. <u>They're</u> in the basement. In the laundry room <u>are</u> five
       (7)   (8)
washers and five dryers. I never have to wait.

B: <u>There are</u> a lot of people in your building?
   (9)

A: <u>In my building 30 apartments.</u>
     (10)

B: <u>Is a janitor</u> in your building?
   (11)

A: Yes. <u>There's</u> a very good janitor. He keeps the building very clean.
    (12)

B: I suppose this apartment costs a lot.

A: Well, yes. The rent <u>is</u> high. But I share the apartment with my
cousins.   (13)

PART 2 Write the plural form for each noun.

box _____*boxes*_____   month _____   child _____

card _____   match _____   desk _____

foot _____   shelf _____   key _____

potato _____   radio _____   story _____

woman _____   mouse _____   bus _____

PART 3 Fill in the blanks with *there, is, are, it,* or *they* or a combination of more than one of these words.

A: _____*Are there*_____ any museums in Chicago?
      (example)

B: Yes, _____ a lot of museums in Chicago.
            (1)

A: _____ a history museum in Chicago?
      (2)

B: Yes, _____ is.
            (3)

A: Where _____ the history museum?
            (4)

B: _____ near downtown.
      (5)

A: _____ any mummies in this museum?
      (6)

B: Yes, there are. _____ from Egypt.
                        (7)

A: _____ a dinosaur in this museum?
      (8)

B: Yes, there is. _____ on the first floor.
                        (9)

A: How many floors _____ in this museum?
                        (10)

B: _____ two floors and a basement.
      (11)

A: _____ a parking lot near this museum?
      (12)

B: Yes, _____, but _____ not very big.
            (13)   *(14)*

PART 4 Fill in the blanks with *the, a, an, some, any,* or *X* for no article.

A: Do you like your apartment?

B: No, I don't.

A: Why not?

B: There are many reasons. First, I don't like _____*the*_____ janitor.
(example)
He's impolite.

A: Anything else?

B: I want to get _____ dog.
(1)

A: So?

B: It's not permitted. _____ landlord says that _____ dogs
(2)   (3)
make a lot of noise.

A: Can you get _____ cat?
(4)

B: Yes, but I don't like _____ cats.
(5)

A: Is your building quiet?

B: No. There are _____ children in _____ building. When
(6)   (7)
I try to study, I can hear _____ children in the next apartment.
(8)
They watch TV all the time.

A: You need to find _____ new apartment.
(9)

B: I think you're right.

Classroom Activities

1. Make a list of things you have, things you don't have but would like to have, and things you don't need. Choose from the list below and add any other items you can think of. Then find a partner and compare lists.

a computer	a house	a credit card
a DVD player	a diamond ring	a speaker phone
a digital camera	a CD player	a cell phone
an encyclopedia	an electric can opener	a big-screen TV
a pager	a microwave oven	a letter opener
an electric toothbrush	a waterbed	a blow dryer
a scale	an electronic calendar	an orange juice squeezer

I have:	I don't have, but I would like to have:	I don't need:

Discuss your chart with a partner. Tell why you need or don't need some things. Tell why you want some things that you don't have.

2. People often use the newspaper to look for an apartment. The Sunday newspaper has the most ads. Bring in a copy of the Sunday newspaper. Look at the section of the newspaper that has apartments for rent. Ask the teacher to help you understand the abbreviations.

3. What other sections are there in the Sunday newspaper? Work with a partner and make a list of everything you can find in the Sunday paper.

   EXAMPLE There's a TV schedule for this week's programs.
   There are a lot of ads and coupons.
   There's a crossword puzzle.

4. Look at the information about two apartments for rent below. What are some of the advantages and disadvantages of each one? Discuss your answers with a partner or with the entire class.

Apartment 1	Apartment 2
a view of a park	on a busy street
rent = $950	rent = $750
fifth floor (an elevator in the building)	third floor walk-up
a new kitchen with a dishwasher	old appliances in the kitchen
pets not allowed	pets allowed
hardwood floors	a carpet in the living room
the janitor lives in the building	the owner lives in the building on the first floor
management controls the heat	the tenant controls the heat
no air conditioners	air conditioners in the bedroom and living room
faces north only	faces east, south, and west
a one-year lease	no lease
a large building—50 apartments	a small building—6 apartments
washers and dryers on each floor	a laundry room in the basement
parking spaces on first-come, first-served basis	a parking space for each tenant

5. Do you have a picture of your house, apartment, or apartment building? Bring it to class and tell about it.

6. Find a partner and pretend that one of you is looking for an apartment and the other person is the landlady, landlord, or manager. Ask and answer questions about the apartment, the building, parking, laundry, and rent. Write your conversation. Then read it to the class.

7. In a small group or with the entire class, discuss the following:
   a. How do people rent apartments in your hometown? Is rent high? Is heat usually included in the rent? Does the landlord usually live in the building?
   b. What are some differences between a typical apartment in this city and a typical apartment in your hometown?

8. Use the plural form of the word in parentheses ( ) to make a generalization. Remember, don't use an article with the plural form to make a generalization. You may work with a partner.

EXAMPLES   (child)

Children like to watch cartoons.

American (highway)

American highways are in good condition.

1. (American)
2. American (child)
3. big (city) in the U.S.
4. (teacher) at this college
5. (student) at this college
6. American (doctor)
7. old (person) in the U.S.
8. American (woman)

Write About it

1. Write a description of a room or place that you like very much. (Review prepositions in Lesson 1.)

EXAMPLE   My favorite place is my living room. There are many pictures on the walls. There's a picture of my grand-parents above the sofa. There are a lot of pictures of my children on the wall next to the sofa.

There's a TV in the corner. Under the TV there is a DVD player. There's a box of movies next to the DVD player . . . .

2. Write a comparison of your apartment in this city and your apartment or house in your hometown.

EXAMPLE   There are many differences between my apartment here and my apartment in Kiev, Ukraine. In my Kiev apartment, there is a door on every room. In my apartment here, only the bedrooms and bathrooms have doors. In my Kiev apartment, there is a small window inside each large window. In the winter, I can open this small window to get some fresh air. My apartment here doesn't have this small window. I have to open the whole window to get air. Sometimes the room becomes too cold. . . .

Internet Activities

Use the Internet to look for apartments for rent and houses for sale in this city (or nearby suburbs). What parts of this city or the suburbs have the highest rents and housing prices?

Additional Activities at http://elt.thomson.com/gic

LESSON

5

GRAMMAR

Possession
Object Pronouns
Questions About the Subject

CONTEXT: Families and Names

Names
William Madison's Name
Who Helps Your Parents?

1. What is your complete name? What do your friends call you?

2. Do you like your name?

Read the following article. Pay special attention to possessive forms.

Americans usually have three names: a first name, a middle name, and a last name (or surname). For example: Marilyn Sue Ellis or Edward David Orleans. Some people use an initial when they sign **their** names: Marilyn S. Ellis, Edward D. Orleans. Not everyone has a middle name.

American women often change **their** last names when they get married. For example, if Marilyn Ellis marries Edward Orleans, **her** name becomes Marilyn Orleans. Not all women follow this custom. Sometimes a woman keeps **her** maiden name[1] and adds **her husband's** name, with or without a hyphen (-): For example, Marilyn Ellis-Orleans or Marilyn Ellis Orleans. Sometimes a woman does not use **her husband's** name at all. In this case, if the couple has children, they have to decide if **their** children will use **their father's** name, **their mother's** name, or both. A man does not usually change **his** name when he gets married.

Some people have **their mother's** last name as a middle name: John Fitzgerald Kennedy, Franklin Delano Roosevelt.[2]

Did You Know?

The five most common last names in the U.S. are Smith, Johnson, Williams, Jones, and Brown.

[1] A *maiden name* is a woman's family name before she gets married.
[2] These are the names of two American presidents.

5.1 | Possessive Form of Nouns

We use the possessive form to show ownership or relationship.

Noun	Ending	Examples
Singular Noun father mother dog	Add apostrophe + *s*	I use my **father's** last name. I don't use my **mother's** last name. My **dog's** name is PeeWee.
Plural Noun Ending in -*s* parents boys	Add apostrophe only	My **parents'** names are Ethel and Herman. My **sons'** names are Ted and Mike.
Irregular Plural Noun children women	Add apostrophe + *s*	What are your **children's** names? Marilyn and Sandra are **women's** names.
Names That End in -*s* Mr. Harris Charles	Add apostrophe only OR Add apostrophe + *s*	Do you know **Charles'** wife? OR Do you know **Charles's** wife?
Inanimate Objects the classroom the school	Use "*the* _____ *of* _____." Do not use apostrophe + *s*.	**The door of the classroom** is closed. Washington College is **the name of my school.**

EXERCISE **1** Fill in the blanks with the possessive form of a noun to make a true statement.

EXAMPLE I use my _____*father's*_____ last name.

1. I use my _____ last name.

2. I don't use my _____ last name.

3. An American married woman often uses her _____ last name.

4. A married woman in my native culture uses her _____ last name.

5. A single American woman usually uses her _____ last name.

6. An American man rarely uses his _____ last name.

7. John Kennedy had his _____ maiden name as a middle name.

Some of the following sentences can show possession with *'s* or *'*. Rewrite these sentences. Write "no change" for the others.

EXAMPLES The teacher knows the names of the students.

The teacher knows the students' names.
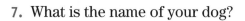

The door of the classroom is usually closed.

No change.

1. The teacher always corrects the homework of the students.

_____

2. The name of the textbook is *Grammar in Context*.

_____

3. The job of the teacher is to explain the grammar.

_____

4. What are the names of your parents?

_____

5. The color of this book is blue.

_____

6. Do you use the last name of your father?

_____

7. What is the name of your dog?

_____

8. The names of the children are Jason and Jessica.

_____

5.2 | Possessive Adjectives

Possessive adjectives show ownership or relationship.

Examples	Explanation
Compare subject pronouns and possessive adjectives	Subject Pronouns — Possessive Adjectives
I like **my** name.	I — my
You're a new student. What's **your** name?	you — your
He likes **his** name.	he — his
She doesn't like **her** name.	she — her
Is this your dog? Is *it* friendly? What's **its** name?	it — its
We use **our** nicknames.	we — our
They are my friends. **Their** last name is Jackson.	they — their
Be careful not to confuse *his* and *her*. My **sister** loves **her** husband. My **uncle** lives with **his** daughter.	*Wrong:* My sister loves *his* husband. *Wrong:* My uncle lives with *her* daughter.
My sister's name is Marilyn. **Her son's** name is David.	We can use a possessive adjective (*my, her*) and a possessive noun (*sister's, son's*) together.
My **sister's husband's** name is Edward.	We can use two possessive nouns together (*sister's husband's*).

EXERCISE 3 Fill in the blanks with the possessive adjective that relates to the subject.

EXAMPLE   I like ____*my*____ teacher.

1. He loves _____ mother.

2. She loves _____ father.

3. A dog loves _____ master.

4. Many American women change _____ names when they get married.

5. Sometimes a woman keeps _____ maiden name and adds _____ husband's name.

6. American men don't usually change _____ names when they get married.

7. Do you use _____ father's last name?

8. I bring _____ book to class.

9. We use _____ books in class.

10. The teacher brings _____ book to class.

11. Some students do _____ homework in the library.

5.3 | Questions with *Whose*

Whose + noun asks about possession or ownership.

Questions	Answers
Whose + noun + aux. verb + subject + verb	
Whose name do you use?	I use **my father's** name.
Whose composition do you like?	I like **Lisa's** composition.
Whose + noun + *be* verb + subject	
Whose book is that?	It's **Bob's** book.
Whose glasses are those?	They're **my** glasses.

EXERCISE 4   Write a question with *whose* and the words given. Answer with the words in parentheses ( ).

EXAMPLES   wife / that (Robert)

Whose wife is that? That's Robert's wife. _____

children / these (Robert)

Whose children are these? These are Robert's children. _____

1. office / this (the dean)

   _____

2. offices / those (the teachers)

   _____

3. dictionary / that (the teacher)

   _____

4. books / those (the students)

   _____

5. car / that (my parents)

   _____

6. house / this (my cousin)

   _____

7. papers / those (Mr. Ross)

   _____

8. CDs / these (the programmer)

   _____

5.4 | Possessive Pronouns

We use possessive pronouns to avoid repetition of a noun.

Examples	Explanation
You don't know my name. I know **yours.** (*yours = your name*) Your name is easy for Americans. **Mine** is hard. (*mine = my name*) My parents are in the U.S. **Theirs** are in Russia. (*theirs = their parents*)	When we omit the noun, we use the possessive pronoun. **Compare:** <table><tr><td>**Possessive Adjectives**</td><td>**Possessive Pronouns**</td></tr><tr><td>my</td><td>mine</td></tr><tr><td>your</td><td>yours</td></tr><tr><td>his</td><td>his</td></tr><tr><td>her</td><td>hers</td></tr><tr><td>our</td><td>ours</td></tr><tr><td>their</td><td>theirs</td></tr></table>
Robert's wife speaks English. **Peter's** doesn't. (*Peter's = Peter's wife*)	After a possessive noun, we can omit the noun.

EXERCISE 5 In each pair of sentences below, replace the underlined words with a possessive pronoun.

EXAMPLE Your book is new. <u>My book</u> is old.
Your book is new. Mine is old.

1. His name is Charles. <u>Her name</u> is Paula.

2. My teacher comes from Houston. <u>Paula's teacher</u> comes from El Paso.

3. I like my English teacher. Does your brother like <u>his English teacher</u>?

4. I have my dictionary today. Do you have <u>your dictionary</u>?

5. Please let me use your book. I don't have <u>my book</u> today.

6. My parents' apartment is big. <u>Our apartment</u> is small.

7. My car is old. <u>Your car</u> is new.

EXERCISE 6 Circle the correct word in parentheses ( ) to complete this conversation.

A: Do you live with ((your,) yours) parents?
(example)

B: No, I don't. Do you live with (your, yours)?
(1)

A: No. I live with (my, mine) sister. (Our, Ours) parents are back
(2)   (3)

home. They live with (my, mine) brother.
(4)

B: (Your, Yours) brother is single, then?
(5)

A: No, he's married. He lives with his wife and (our, ours) parents.
(6)

B: If he's married, why does he live with (your, yours) parents?
(7)

A: In (our, ours) country, it's an honor to live with parents.
(8)

B: Not in (my, mine). Grown children don't usually want to live with
(9)

(their, theirs) parents, and parents don't usually want to live with
(10)

(their, theirs) grown children.
(11)

A: Where do (your, yours) parents live?
(12)

B: They live in another state.

A: Isn't that hard for you?

B: Not really. I have (my, mine) own life, and they have (their, theirs).
(13)   (14)

5.5 | The Subject and the Object

Examples	Explanation
S V O Bob likes Mary. We like movies.	The **subject** (S) comes before the verb (V). The **object** (O) comes after the verb. The object is a person or a thing.
S V O S V O Bob likes Mary because **she** helps **him**. ↑ ↑ ↑ ↑ **S V O S V O** I like movies because **they** entertain **me**. ↑ ↑ ↑ ↑	We can use pronouns for the **subject** and the **object.**

Before You Read

1. What are common American names?

2. What is a very common first name in your country or native culture? What is a very common last name? Is your name common in your country or native culture?

Read the following conversation. Pay special attention to object pronouns.

A: I have many questions about American names. Can you answer **them** for me?

B: Of course.

A: Tell **me** about your name.

B: My name is William, but my friends call **me** Bill.

A: Why do they call **you** Bill?

B: Bill is a common nickname for William.

A: Is William your first name?

B: Yes.

A: What's your full name?

B: William Michael Madison.

A: Do you ever use your middle name?

B: I only use **it** for very formal occasions. I sign my name William M. Madison, Jr. (junior).

A: What does "junior" mean?

B: It means that **I** have the same name as my father. His name is William Madison, Sr. (senior).

A: What's your wife's name?

B: Anna Marie Simms-Madison. I call **her** Annie.

A: Why does she have two last names?

B: Simms is her father's last name, and Madison is mine. She uses both names with a hyphen (-) between **them.**

A: Do you have any children?

B: Yes. We have a son and a daughter. Our son's name is Richard, but we call **him** Dick. Our daughter's name is Elizabeth, but everybody calls **her** Lizzy.

A: What do your children call **you**?

B: They call **us** Mommy and Daddy, of course.

5.6 | Object Pronouns

Subject		Object	Examples		
			Subject	Verb	Object
I	⟶	me	You	love	me.
you	⟶	you	I	love	you.
he	⟶	him	She	loves	him.
she	⟶	her	He	loves	her.
it	⟶	it	We	love	it.
we	⟶	us	They	love	us.
they	⟶	them	We	love	them.

They love us

He loves her

We can use an object pronoun after the verb or after a preposition.		
Object Noun	**Object Pronoun**	**Explanation**
I have a **middle name.**	I use **it** when I sign my name.	We can use an object pronoun to substitute for an object noun.
He loves **his wife.**	The kids love **her** too.	
You know **my son.**	Friends call **him** Dick.	
We have **two children.**	We love **them.**	We use *them* for plural people and things.
I need **my books.**	I use **them** in class.	
I have **two last names.**	I use both *of* **them.**	An object pronoun can follow a preposition (*of, about, to, from, in,* etc.).
My sister has **a son.**	She always talks *about* **him.**	

EXERCISE 7   Fill in the blanks. Substitute an object pronoun for the underlined words.

EXAMPLE   I look like <u>my father</u>, but my brother doesn't look like ____*him*____.

1. <u>My brother's</u> name is William, but we call _____ Bill.
2. <u>I</u> understand the teacher, and the teacher understands _____.
3. I use <u>my dictionary</u> when I write, but I don't use _____ when I speak.
4. I like <u>this city</u>. Do you like _____ too?
5. I talk to <u>Americans</u>, but I don't always understand _____.
6. We listen to <u>the teacher</u>, and we talk to _____.
7. When <u>we</u> make a mistake, the teacher corrects _____.
8. <u>The president</u> has advisers. They help _____ make decisions.
9. <u>You</u> understand me, and I understand _____.
10. <u>My friends</u> sometimes visit me, and I sometimes visit _____.

EXERCISE 8   This is a conversation between two students, one from China (A), one from the U.S. (B). Fill in the blanks with an appropriate object pronoun.

A: Americans are very informal about names. The teacher calls

_____*us*_____ by our first names.
     (example)

B: What does the teacher call _____ in your country?
                                        (1)

A: In my country, when a teacher talks to a woman, he calls

_____ "Miss" or "Madam." When he talks to a man, he calls
     (2)

_____ "Sir."
     (3)

B: I like it when the teacher calls _____ by my first name.
                                              (4)

A: I don't. There's another strange thing: In my country, we never use a

first name for our teachers. We call _____ "Professor" or
                                            (5)

"Teacher." Our teacher here gets mad when we call _____
                                                         (6)

"Teacher." She doesn't like _____. She says it's impolite. But in
                                  (7)

my country, "Teacher" is a term of great respect.

B: Only small children in the U.S. call their teacher "Teacher." If you

know your teacher's name, use _____.
                                     (8)

A: Do you mean I should call _____ Dawn?
(9)

B: If that's what she likes.

A: I'm sorry. I can't do _____. She's about 50 years old, and
(10)
I'm only 20.

B: Then call _____ Ms. Paskow.
(11)

A: She doesn't like to use her last name. She says everyone

mispronounces _____. Sometimes I call _____ Ms. Dawn, but
(12)   (13)
she says no one does that here.

B: We have an expression, "When in Rome, do as the Romans do."[3]

A: It's hard for _____ to change my customs after a lifetime of
(14)
following _____.
(15)

EXERCISE 9 Fill in the blanks with *I*, *I'm*, *my*, *mine*, or *me*.

EXAMPLES _____*I'm*_____ a foreign student. _____*I*_____ come from Japan.

_____*My*_____ roommate's parents live in the U.S., but _____*mine*_____ live in

Japan. _____*My*_____ parents write to _____*me*_____ twice a month.

1. _____ roommate's name is Kelly. _____ is Yuki.

2. _____ roommate helps _____ with my English.

3. _____ study at the University of Wisconsin.

4. _____ major is engineering.

5. _____ have a roommate.

6. _____ 20 years old.

7. _____ parents don't live in
the U.S.

[3] This expression means that you should follow the customs of the country you are in.

EXERCISE 10   Fill in the blanks with *he*, *he's*, *his*, or *him*.

EXAMPLE   I have a good friend. _____*His*_____ name is Paul. _____*He's*_____ Puerto Rican. _____*He*_____ lives in New York. I like _____*him*_____.

1. _____ married.
2. _____ works in an office.
3. _____ an accountant.
4. _____ son helps _____ in _____ business.
5. _____ 37 years old. _____ wife is 35.
6. My wife and _____ wife are friends.
7. My wife is a doctor. _____ is a computer programmer.

EXERCISE 11   Fill in the blanks with *she*, *she's*, *her*, or *hers*.

EXAMPLE   I have a friend. _____*Her*_____ name's Diane. _____*She's*_____ American. _____*She*_____ lives in Boston. My native language is Korean. _____*Hers*_____ is English.

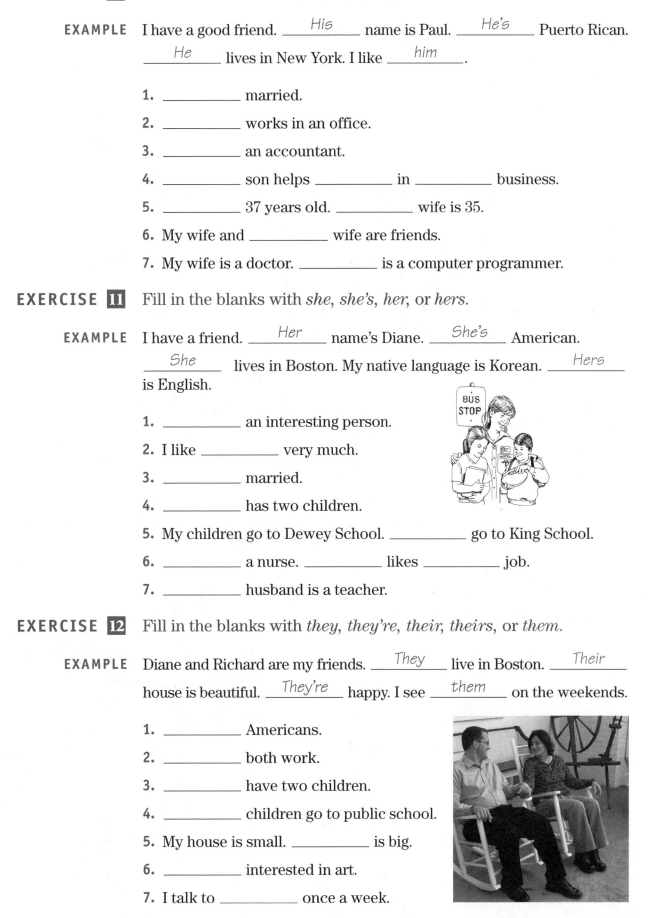

1. _____ an interesting person.
2. I like _____ very much.
3. _____ married.
4. _____ has two children.
5. My children go to Dewey School. _____ go to King School.
6. _____ a nurse. _____ likes _____ job.
7. _____ husband is a teacher.

EXERCISE 12   Fill in the blanks with *they*, *they're*, *their*, *theirs*, or *them*.

EXAMPLE   Diane and Richard are my friends. _____*They*_____ live in Boston. _____*Their*_____ house is beautiful. _____*They're*_____ happy. I see _____*them*_____ on the weekends.

1. _____ Americans.
2. _____ both work.
3. _____ have two children.
4. _____ children go to public school.
5. My house is small. _____ is big.
6. _____ interested in art.
7. I talk to _____ once a week.

EXERCISE 13 Fill in the blanks about a cat. Use *it, it's,* or *its.*

EXAMPLE ___It's___ an independent animal. ___It___ always lands on ___its___ feet.

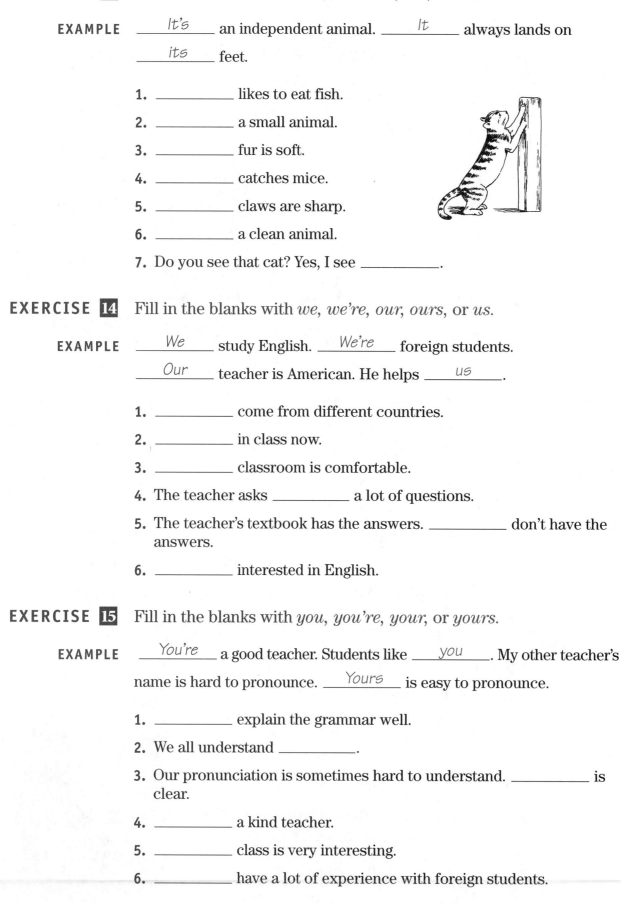

1. _____ likes to eat fish.

2. _____ a small animal.

3. _____ fur is soft.

4. _____ catches mice.

5. _____ claws are sharp.

6. _____ a clean animal.

7. Do you see that cat? Yes, I see _____.

EXERCISE 14 Fill in the blanks with *we, we're, our, ours,* or *us.*

EXAMPLE ___We___ study English. ___We're___ foreign students.

___Our___ teacher is American. He helps ___us___.

1. _____ come from different countries.

2. _____ in class now.

3. _____ classroom is comfortable.

4. The teacher asks _____ a lot of questions.

5. The teacher's textbook has the answers. _____ don't have the answers.

6. _____ interested in English.

EXERCISE 15 Fill in the blanks with *you, you're, your,* or *yours.*

EXAMPLE ___You're___ a good teacher. Students like ___you___. My other teacher's name is hard to pronounce. ___Yours___ is easy to pronounce.

1. _____ explain the grammar well.

2. We all understand _____.

3. Our pronunciation is sometimes hard to understand. _____ is clear.

4. _____ a kind teacher.

5. _____ class is very interesting.

6. _____ have a lot of experience with foreign students.

Before You Read

1. At what age should adult children leave home if they're not married?

2. Should adult children take care of their parents?

🎧 Read the following conversation. Pay special attention to questions.

A: **Where does your dad live?**

B: He lives back in our country.

A: Is he in good health?

B: His health is so-so.

A: **Who takes care of him?**

B: My brother and his wife do.

A: Do they go to his house every day?

B: No. They live with him.

A: **Why do they live with him?**

B: It's the custom in my country. What about in America? Do you live with your parents?

A: Of course not. I'm 25. I live with my roommate.

B: **Where do your parents live?**

A: My parents are divorced. My mother lives just a couple of miles from me. My dad lives in another state.

B: **How often do you see your parents?**

A: I see my dad a couple of times a year. I see my mom about once or twice a month.

B: Is that all? **Who helps them? Who shops for them? Who cooks for them?**

A: They're in their 60s and in great health. They can do everything. No one takes care of them. **What's wrong with that?**

B: What about when they get older?

A: I never think about it. **Who knows about the future?** I have my life to live, and they have theirs.

5.7 | Questions About the Subject or About the Complement

Compare these statements and related questions about the complement:

Subject	Verb	Complement	Wh-Word	Does/Do	Subject	Verb	
Dad	lives	in Korea.	Where	does	Dad	live?	We use *do* and *does* to ask a question about the complement of the sentence.
Dad	lives	with someone.	Who(m)	does	he	live with?	
I	visit	once a month.	When	do	you	visit?	

Compare these statements and related questions about the subject:

Subject	Verb	Who/What	Verb -s Form		
Someone	helps my father.	Who	helps	your father?	When we ask a question about the subject, we don't use *do* or *does*. We can use the *-s* form in the question.
Nobody	knows.	Who	knows	about the future?	
Something is wrong.		What	is	wrong with that?	

EXERCISE 16 ABOUT YOU Talk about some jobs in your house. Ask another student, "Who _____s in your house?" The other student will answer.

EXAMPLES take out the garbage
  A: Who takes out the garbage in your house?
  B: My brother does.

vacuum the carpet
  A: Who vacuums the carpet in your house?
  B: Nobody does. We don't have carpets.

1. dust the furniture
2. shop for groceries
3. pay the bills
4. wash the dishes
5. make your bed

6. vacuum the carpet
7. wash the clothes
8. cook the meals
9. sweep the floor

EXERCISE 17 Fill in the blanks to complete this conversation.

A: ___*Do you like*___ going to school in the U.S.?
      (example)

B: Yes, I like it very much. But I miss my parents.

A: Where ___*do they live*___?
            (example)

B: They live in Peru.

A: How old ___are they___ ?
  (example)

B: They're in their 60s.

A: Who _____ of them?
  (1)

B: No one takes care of them. They're in great health.

A: _____ alone?
  (2)

B: No, they don't. They live with my oldest sister.

A: _____ ?
  (3)

B: No, she isn't single. She's married. She's a nurse and her husband is a doctor.

A: How many _____ ?
  (4)

B: They have three kids. The girl is seven, and the boys are six and two.

A: Who _____ the kids when your sister and her husband go to work?
  (5)

B: The older two are in school. My parents take care of the youngest boy.

A: How often _____ your parents?
  (6)

B: I talk to them about once a week.

A: Is it expensive to call your country?

B: Not really. I buy a phone card.

A: How much _____ ?
  (7)

B: It costs $5.00 We can talk for 30 minutes.

A: Do you plan to see them soon?

B: Who _____ ? Maybe yes, maybe no. I hope so.
  (8)

5.8 | Who, Whom, Who's, Whose

Examples	Explanation
Compare:	
Who needs the teacher's help? We do.	*Who* = Subject
Who(m)* do you love? I love my parents.	*Who(m)* = Object
Who's that man? He's my dad.	*Who's* = Who is
Whose book is this? It's mine.	*Whose* = Possession (ownership)

*Note: Many native speakers use *who* in place of *whom*.

EXERCISE 18 Fill in the blanks with *who*, *whom*, *who's*, or *whose*.

EXAMPLE <u> Who </u> likes ice cream? I like ice cream.

1. _____ last name do you use? I use my father's last name.

2. _____ composition is this? It doesn't have a name on it. It's mine.

3. _____ is your best friend? My best friend is Nina.

4. _____ has my dictionary? I do. Do you need it now?

5. _____ do you call when you have a problem? I call my parents.

6. _____ needs more practice with pronouns? We all do!

EXERCISE 19 *Combination exercise.* Circle the correct word to complete this conversation between two students.

EXAMPLE **A:** (Who, (Who's,) Whose, Whom) your English teacher?
(example)

B: (My, Mine, Me) teacher's name is Charles Flynn.
(1)

A: (My, Mine, Me) is Marianne Peters. She's Mr. Flynn's wife.
(2)

B: Oh, really? His last name is different from (she, her, hers).
(3)

A: Yes. She uses (her, hers, his, he's) father's last name, not her
(4)

(husband's, husbands', husbands, husband).
(5)

B: Do they have children?

A: Yes.

B: (Whose, Who's, Who, Whom) name do the children use?
(6)

A: (They, They're, Their, Theirs) children use both last names.
(7)

B: How do you know so much about (you, you're, your, yours) teacher
(8)

and (she, she's, her, hers) children?
(9)

A: We talk about (we, us, our, ours) names in class. We also talk about
(10)

American customs. She explains her customs, and we explain
(our, ours, us).
(11)

B: Mr. Flynn doesn't talk about (her, his, he's, hers) family in class.
(12)

A: Do you call (her, his, him, he) "mister"?
(13)

B: Of course. (He, He's, His) the teacher. We show respect.
(14)

A: But we call Marianne by (her, hers, she) first name. (She, She's, Her)
(15) (16)

prefers that.

B: I prefer to call (our, us, ours) teachers by (they, they're, their, theirs)
(17) (18)

last names. That's the way we do it in my country.

A: And in (me, my, mine) too. But (we, we're, us) in the U.S. now.
(19) (20)

There's an expression: When in Rome, do as the Romans do.

SUMMARY OF LESSON 5

1. Pronouns and Possessive Forms

Subject Pronoun	Object Pronoun	Possessive Adjective	Possessive Pronoun
I	me	my	mine
you	you	your	yours
he	him	his	his
she	her	her	hers
it	it	its	—
we	us	our	ours
they	them	their	theirs
who	whom	whose	whose

Subject	**I** come from Cuba	**They** come from Korea.	**Who** comes from Poland?
Object	The teacher helps **me**.	The teacher helps **them**.	**Who(m)** does the teacher help?
Possessive Adjective	**My** name is Rosa.	**Their** names are Kim and Park.	**Whose** name do you use?
Possessive Pronoun	Your book is new. **Mine** is used.	Your book is new. **Theirs** is used.	This is your book. **Whose** is that?

2. Possessive Forms of Nouns
  Jack's car is old.
  His **parents'** car is new.
  The **children's** toys are on the floor.
  What's the name of **our textbook?**

1. Don't confuse *you're* (you are) and *your* (possessive form).

   You're
   ~~Your~~ a good person.

   your
   Where's ~~you're~~ book?

2. Don't confuse *he's* (he is) and *his* (possessive form).

   His
   ~~He's~~ name is Paul.

   He's
   ~~His~~ a good student.

3. Don't confuse *it's* (it is) and *its* (possessive form).

   It's
   ~~Its~~ a beautiful day today.

   its
   A monkey uses ~~it's~~ tail to climb trees.

4. Don't confuse *his* (masculine) and *her* (feminine).

   his
   My brother loves ~~her~~ daughter.

   her
   My sister loves ~~his~~ son.

5. Don't confuse *my* and *mine*.

   my
   I don't have ~~mine~~ book today.

6. Don't confuse *they're* and *their*.

   Their
   I have two American friends. ~~They're~~ names are Bob and Sue.

7. Use the correct pronoun (subject or object).

   her
   I have a daughter. I love ~~she~~ very much.

   I
   My father and ~~me~~ like to go fishing.

8. Don't use *the* with a possessive form.

   M
   ~~The~~ ~~m~~y friend is very tall.

   I need ~~the~~ your dictionary.

9. Don't use *do* or *does* in a *who* question about the subject.

   has
   Who ~~does have~~ a Spanish dictionary?

10. Don't separate *whose* from the noun.

    book
    Whose ˄ is this ~~book~~?

11. Don't confuse *whose* and *who's*.

    Whose
    ~~Who's~~ coat is that?

12. Use the correct word order for possession.

    My neighbor's dog
    ~~Dog my neighbor~~ makes a lot of noise.

13. Put the apostrophe in the right place.

    parents'
    My ~~parent's~~ car is new.

14. Don't use the possessive form for nonliving things.

    name of the book
    Grammar in Context is the ~~book's name~~.

LESSON 5 TEST/REVIEW

PART 1 Find the mistakes with the underlined words and correct them. Not every sentence has a mistake. If the sentence is correct, write *C*.

Whose
EXAMPLES ~~Who's~~ book is that?

Who's your best friend?   *C*

1. Where does <u>you're</u> brother live?

2. Paul is in my English class, but <u>his</u> not in my math class.

3. <u>Its</u> important to know a second language.

4. <u>Whose</u> name do you use, your <u>father's</u> or your <u>mother's</u>?

5. <u>Who wants</u> to leave early today? We all do.

6. Maria's son goes to a bilingual school. <u>Her son's teacher</u> comes from Cuba.

7. I visit my girlfriend once a week. <u>His</u> son likes to play with <u>mine</u>.

8. <u>The door of the classroom</u> is open.

9. Do you know <u>the first name the teacher</u>?

10. I have two married brothers. <u>My brother's wives</u> are wonderful women.

11. <u>Your</u> always late to class.

12. <u>My the brother's</u> car is new.

13. <u>Whose is this umbrella</u>?

14. She likes her mother-in-law because <u>mother her husband</u> always helps her.

15. Do they visit <u>theirs</u> parents often?

16. A dog wags (moves) <u>its</u> tail when <u>it's</u> happy.

17. Susan and Linda are <u>women's</u> names.

18. <u>Who does have</u> a red pen?

19. <u>My friend and me</u> eat dinner together once a week.

20. <u>Whose pen</u> is this?

PART 2   Choose the correct word to complete these sentences.

EXAMPLE   Most American women change _____ *c* _____ names when they get married, but not all do.

    a. her   **b.** hers   **c.** their   **d.** theirs

1. I have two _____.
    a. sisters   **b.** sister's   **c.** sisters'   **d.** sister

2. _____ names are Marilyn and Charlotte.
    a. Their   **b.** Theirs   **c.** They're   **d.** They   **e.** Hers

3. _____ both married.
    a. Their   **b.** They're   **c.** They   **d.** Them   **e.** There

4. Marilyn uses _____.
    a. the last name her husband
    b. the last name of his husband
    c. her husband's last name
    d. his husband's last name

5. Charlotte uses _____ father's last name.
   a. we   **b.** our   **c.** ours   **d.** us

6. I have one brother. _____ married.
   a. He's   **b.** His   **c.** He   **d.** Him

7. _____ wife is very nice.
   a. Him   **b.** Her   **c.** His   **d.** He's

8. _____ first name is Sandra.
   a. My   **b.** Mine   **c.** I'm   **d.** Me

9. My friends call _____ "Sandy."
   a. me   **b.** my   **c.** mine

10. My sister often uses her middle name, but I rarely use _____.
    a. my   **b.** mine   **c.** me   **d.** I'm

11. You have a dog, but I don't know _____ name.
    a. it   **b.** it's   **c.** its

12. _____ your teacher?
    a. Whom   **b.** Who   **c.** Whose   **d.** Who's

13. Her _____ names are Ricky and Eddie.
    a. childs'   **b.** children's   **c.** childrens   **d.** childrens'

14. _____ has the newspaper?
    a. Whom   **b.** Whose   **c.** Who   **d.** Who's

15. Who _____ more time with the test?
    a. need   **b.** does need   **c.** needs   **d.** does needs

16. The teacher's name is on _____.
    a. the door of her office
    b. her office's door
    c. the door her office
    d. her the office's door

17. _____
    a. Who's is that office?
    b. Whose is that office?
    c. Who's office is that?
    d. Whose office is that?

PART 3 Two women are talking about names. Fill in the blanks with possessive forms, subject pronouns, or object pronouns. Some blanks need an apostrophe or an apostrophe + *s*.

A: What's your last name?

B: It's Woods.

A: Woods sounds like an American name. But ___*you're*___ Polish, aren't you?
(example)

B: Yes, but Americans have trouble pronouncing _____ name, so I use the name "Woods."
(1)

A: What's _____ real last name?
(2)

B: Wodzianicki.

A: My name is hard for Americans too, but _____ like my
(3)
name, and I don't want to change _____. I'm proud of it.
(4)

B: What's _____ last name?
(5)

A: Lopez Hernandez.

B: Why do _____ have two last names?
(6)

A: I come from Mexico. Mexicans have two last names. Mexicans use both parents _____ names.
(7)

B: What happens when a woman get married? Does she use _____
(8)
parent _____ names and _____ husband _____
(9)   *(10)*   *(11)*
name too?

A: No. When a woman gets married, she usually drops _____
(12)
mother _____ name. She adds "of" (in Spanish, "de") and
(13)
_____ husband _____ name. My sister is married.
(14)   *(15)*
_____ name is Maria Lopez de Castillo. Lopez is _____
(16)   *(17)*
father _____ name and Castillo is her husband _____
(18)   *(19)*
name. _____ kids _____ last name is Castillo Lopez.
(20)   *(21)*

B: That's confusing. Everybody in the family has a different last name.

A: It's not confusing for us. You understand your customs, and we understand _____.
(22)

B: Do your sister _____ kids have American first names?
(23)

A: My sister gave _____ Spanish names, but _____ friends
(24)   (25)

gave them American names. Her daughter _____ name is Rosa,
(26)

but _____ friends call her Rose. _____ son _____
(27)   (28)   (29)

name is Eduardo, but _____ friends call _____
(30)   (31)

Eddie. Ricardo is the youngest one. _____ still a baby, but
(32)

when he goes to school, _____ friends will probably call
(33)

_____ Rick.
(34)

EXPANSION ACTIVITIES

Classroom Activities

1. Find a partner. Compare yourself to your partner. Compare physical characteristics, clothes, family, home, job, car, and so on. Report some interesting facts to the class.

   EXAMPLE My hair is straight. Mark's is curly.
   His eyes are blue. Mine are brown.
   My family lives in this city. Mark's family lives in Romania.

2. One student will ask these *who* questions. Raise your hand if this is a fact about you. The first student will answer the question after he or she sees raised hands.

   EXAMPLE Who has kids?
   Ben, Maria, and Lidia have kids.
   Who has a cell phone?
   No one has a cell phone.

   1. Who has kids?

   2. Who likes cartoons?

   3. Who plays soccer?

   4. Who has a laptop computer?

5. Who is a sports fan?

6. Who likes to swim?

7. Who is a vegetarian?

8. Who wants a grammar test?

9. Who has American friends?

10. Who has a pet?

11. Who lives in a house?

12. Who is over 6 feet tall?

13. Who has a motorcycle?

14. Who has an e-mail address?

15. Who gets a lot of junk mail?

16. Who exercises every day?

17. Who watches TV in the morning?

18. Who has a middle name?

19. Who wants to become an American citizen?

20. Who plays a musical instrument?

3. Think of something unusual that you do or are. Write a sentence telling what you do or are. Then ask a question to find out who else does or is this.

EXAMPLES   I have a pet snake. Who else has a pet snake?
I play volleyball. Who else plays volleyball?
I am a Buddhist. Who else is a Buddhist?

(Variation: On a piece of paper, write something unusual that you do or are. Give the papers to the teacher. The teacher reads a statement. Other students—and the teacher—try to guess who wrote it. Example: Someone has a pet snake. Who has a pet snake?)

4. Discuss naming customs in your native culture. Do people have a middle name? Do fathers and sons ever have the same name? Tell about your name. Does it mean something?

Joke

A woman is outside her house. A dog is near her. A man walks by and is interested in the dog. He wants to pet the dog. He asks the woman, "Does your dog bite?" The woman answers no. The man pets the dog, and the dog bites him. He says, "You told me that your dog doesn't bite." The woman answers, "This is not my dog. Mine is in the house."

Outside Activity

Ask an American to tell you about his or her name. Tell the class something interesting you learned from this American.

Internet Activity

Find a phone directory on the Internet. Look up your last name in a major American city, such as New York City, or in the city where you live. How many people in this city have your last name?

Additional Activities at **http://elt.thomson.com/gic**

LESSON 6

GRAMMAR

The Present Continuous Tense[1]

CONTEXT: Observations About American Life

Observations in the Park
Observations in the School Cafeteria

[1]The present continuous tense is sometimes called the present progressive tense.

Before You Read

1. Do you ever write in a journal?

2. Do you ever compare the behavior of Americans to the behavior of people from your native culture?

Read the following entry from Dan's journal. Pay special attention to the present continuous tense.

September 9

I**'m taking** an ESL course this semester. Our teacher wants us to write in a journal every day. I**'m beginning** my journal now. I'm in the park now. It's a beautiful day. The sun **is shining.** I**'m sitting** on a park bench and **observing** the behavior of people around me.

It's warm and most of the people **are wearing** shorts, but I**'m wearing** long pants. Even old people **are wearing** shorts. This surprises me. Some people **are jogging.** They **are** all **carrying** a personal stereo and **wearing** headphones. They **are** all **jogging** alone. A lot of people **are going** by on rollerskates. Some young kids **are using** a skateboard. It seems that these are popular activities here.

A group of young men **is playing** soccer. I don't think they're Americans. I think Americans don't like soccer. I hear them speaking Spanish. Americans prefer baseball. In another part of the park, small children **are playing** baseball. Their parents **are watching** them. This is called Little League. Little League is very popular here.

One man **is riding** a bike and **talking** on a cell phone at the same time. Some people **are having** a picnic. They **are barbecuing** hamburgers.

There is a group of teenagers nearby. They **are talking** very loudly. They have a big boombox and **are listening** to hip-hop music. They**'re making** a lot of noise.

I**'m learning** a lot about the American lifestyle.

6.1 | The Present Continuous Tense

To form the present continuous tense, use a form of *be* (*is, am, are*) + verb *-ing*. We use the present continuous tense to describe an action in progress at this moment.

Examples	Explanation
Subject **Be** **Verb + -ing** **Complement** I **am** **taking** an ESL class. The sun **is** **shining.** A man **is** **jogging.** He **is** **wearing** shorts. You **are** **reading** Dan's journal. Kids **are** **listening** to music. They **are** **talking** very loudly. We **are** **learning** about American life.	I → am He/She/It → is Singular Subject → is + verb -ing We/You/They → are Plural Subject → are
I'm taking an ESL class this semester. **They're** listening to music. **We're** observing the American lifestyle. **Dan's** writing in his journal.	We can make a contraction with the subject pronoun and a form of *be*. Most nouns can also form a contraction with *is*.[2]

Dan **isn't** writing a composition. He's writing in his journal.
The teenagers **aren't** paying attention to other people.
	To form the negative, put *not* after the verb *am/is/are*.
	Negative contractions:
	    is not = isn't
	    are not = aren't
	There is no contraction for *am not*.

A man **is riding** his bike **and talking** on his cell phone.	When the subject is doing two or more things, we don't repeat the verb *be* after *and*.

EXERCISE **1** Fill in the blanks with the missing part of each sentence.

EXAMPLE I'___*m*___ writing in my journal.

1. Most people are wear _____ shorts.

2. Some young men _____ playing soccer.

3. Some children are play _____ baseball.

4. Teenagers _____ listening to music.

5. I'_____ looking at people in the park.

6. The sun _____ shining.

7. A man is riding his bike and talk _____ on his cell phone.

8. I'm learn _____ about life in the U.S.

[2]See Lesson 1, page 8 for exceptions.

6.2 | Spelling of the *-ing* Form

Rule	Verbs	*-ing* Form
Add *-ing* to most verbs. (Note: Do not drop the *y* of the base form.)	eat go study	eat**ing** go**ing** study**ing**
For a one-syllable verb that ends in a consonant + vowel + consonant (CVC), double the final consonant and add *-ing*.	p l a n ↓ ↓ ↓ C V C s t o p ↓ ↓ ↓ C V C s i t ↓ ↓ ↓ C V C	plan**ning** stop**ping** sit**ting**
Do not double a final *w, x,* or *y*.	show mix stay	show**ing** mix**ing** stay**ing**
For a two-syllable verb that ends in CVC, double the final consonant only if the last syllable is stressed.	refér admít begín	refer**ring** admit**ting** begin**ning**
When the last syllable of a two-syllable verb is not stressed, do not double the final consonant.	lísten ópen óffer	listen**ing** open**ing** offer**ing**
If the verb ends in a consonant + *e,* drop the *e* before adding *-ing*.	live take write	liv**ing** tak**ing** writ**ing**

EXERCISE 2 Write the *-ing* form of the verb. (Two-syllable verbs that end in CVC have accent marks to show which syllable is stressed.)

EXAMPLES play _____*playing*_____

make _____*making*_____

1. plan _____

2. ópen _____

3. sit _____

4. begín _____

5. hurry _____

6. háppen _____

7. stay _____

8. grow _____

9. marry _____

10. grab _____

11. write _____

12. fix _____

13. wipe _____   17. wait _____

14. carry _____   18. serve _____

15. drink _____   19. vísit _____

16. drive _____   20. prefér _____

EXERCISE 3 Fill in the blanks with the present continuous tense of the verb in parentheses ( ). Use correct spelling.

EXAMPLE Dan _____*is observing*_____ people in the park.
(observe)

1. He _____ about his observations.
(write)

2. Some men _____ soccer.
(play)

3. A man _____ a bike.
(ride)

4. Some people _____.
(jog)

5. The sun _____.
(shine)

6. He _____ on a park bench.
(sit)

7. Some people _____ by on rollerskates and skate-boards.
(go)

8. Some people _____ a personal stereo.
(carry)

6.3 | The Present Continuous Tense—Uses

Examples	Explanation
I **am writing** in my journal now. I **am observing** the American lifestyle. Children **are playing** baseball. Teenagers **are listening** to music.	To show that an action is in progress now, at this moment.
I**'m learning** about the American lifestyle. I**'m taking** an ESL course this semester.	To show a long-term action that is in progress. It may not be happening at this exact moment.
Most people **are wearing** shorts. I**'m sitting** on a park bench.	To describe a state or condition, using the following verbs: *sit, stand, wear, sleep*.

EXERCISE 4 ABOUT YOU Make a **true** affirmative statement or negative statement about your activities now with the words given.

EXAMPLES wear a watch
I'm not wearing a watch (now).

drink coffee
I'm drinking coffee (now).

1. sit in the back of the room
2. speak my native language
3. pay attention
4. ask questions
5. learn the present continuous tense

6. look out the window
7. look at the chalkboard
8. write a composition
9. use my textbook
10. wear jeans

EXERCISE 5 ABOUT YOU Make a true affirmative statement or negative statement about yourself with the words given. Talk about a long-term action.

EXAMPLES look for a job
I'm looking for a job.

live in a hotel
I'm not living in a hotel.

1. look for a new apartment
2. learn a lot of English
3. gain weight
4. lose weight
5. spend a lot of money
6. save my money
7. write a term paper[3]
8. try to understand American customs
9. meet Americans
10. learn how to drive
11. live in a dorm
12. plan to return to my hometown

[3]A *term paper* is a paper that students write for class. The student researches a topic. It often takes a student a full semester (or term) to produce this paper.

6.4 | Questions with the Present Continuous Tense

Affirmative Statements and Questions

Wh- Word	Be	Subject	Be	Verb + -ing	Complement	Short Answer
		Dan	is	writing.		
	Is	he		writing	a composition?	No, he isn't.
What	is	he		writing?		A page in his journal.
		The kids	are	playing.		
	Are	they		playing	soccer?	No, they aren't.
What	are	they		playing?		Baseball.

Negative Statements and Questions

Wh- Word	Be + n't	Subject	Be + n't	Verb + -ing	Complement
		The kids	aren't	playing	soccer.
Why	aren't	they		playing	soccer?
		Dan	isn't	using	his computer.
Why	isn't	he		using	his computer?

Language Note:
When the question is "What . . . doing?" we usually answer with a different verb.
> What is Dan **doing?** He's **writing** in his journal.
> What are those kids **doing?** They're **playing** baseball.

EXERCISE 6 Use the words given to ask a question about what this class is doing now. Another student will answer.

EXAMPLE we / use the textbook now
A: Are we using the textbook now?
B: Yes, we are.

1. the teacher / wear a sweater
2. the teacher / write on the chalkboard
3. the teacher / erase the chalkboard
4. the teacher / sit at the desk
5. the teacher / take attendance
6. the teacher / explain the grammar
7. the teacher / help the students
8. we / practice the present continuous tense
9. we / practice the past tense
10. we / review Lesson 5
11. we / make mistakes
12. what / the teacher / wear
13. where / the teacher / stand or sit
14. what exercise / we / do
15. what / you / think about

EXERCISE 7 ABOUT YOU Ask a question about a long-term action with the words given. Another student will answer.

EXAMPLE   you / study math this semester

A: Are you studying math this semester?
B: Yes, I am.

1. you / plan to buy a car
2. you / study biology this semester
3. you / take other courses this semester
4. you / look for a new apartment
5. you / look for a job
6. your English / improve
7. your vocabulary / grow
8. the teacher / help you
9. the students / make progress
10. you / learn about other students' countries

EXERCISE 8 ABOUT YOU Fill in the blanks with *I'm* or *I'm not* + the *-ing* form of the verb in parentheses ( ) to tell if you are doing these things now or at this general point in time. Then ask another student if he or she is doing this activity now. The other student will answer.

EXAMPLES   (plan) _____*I'm planning*_____ to buy a computer.

A: Are you planning to buy a computer?
B: Yes, I am.

(learn) _____*I'm not learning*_____ to drive a car.

A: Are you learning to drive a car?
B: No, I'm not.

1. (wear) _____ jeans.

2. (hold) _____ a pencil.

3. (chew) _____ gum.

4. (think) _____ about the weekend.

5. (live) _____ in a dorm.

6. (plan) _____ to take a vacation.

7. (look) _____ for a job.

8. (plan) _____ to buy a computer.

9. (take) _____ a computer class this semester.

10. (get) _____ tired.

11. (gain) _____ weight.

12. (learn) _____ about the history of the U.S.

13. (learn) _____ how to drive.

EXERCISE 9   ABOUT YOU Read each sentence. Then ask a *wh-* question about the words in parentheses ( ). Another student will answer.

EXAMPLE   We're doing an exercise. (What exercise)
A: What exercise are we doing?
B: We're doing Exercise 9.

1. We're practicing a tense. (What tense)

2. We're using a textbook. (What kind of book)

3. You're listening to the teacher. (Why)

4. The teacher's helping the students. (Why)

5. I'm answering a question. (Which question)

6. We're practicing questions. (What kind of questions)

7. Your English is improving. (Why)

8. Your life is changing. (How)

9. You're taking courses. (How many courses)

EXERCISE 10   A woman is calling her husband from a cell phone in her car. Fill in the blanks to complete the conversation.

A: Hello?
B: Hi. It's Betty.

A: Oh, hi, Betty. This connection is so noisy. Where ___*are you calling*___ from?
                                                              (example)

B: I _____ from the car. I _____
            (1)   (2)
the cell phone.

A: _____ home now?
                        (3)

B: No, I'm not. I'm driving to the airport.

A: Why _____ to the airport?
                        (4)

B: I'm going to pick up a client.
A: I can't hear you. There's so much noise.

B: Airplanes _____ overhead. They're very low.
                        (5)

A: I can't hear you. Talk louder please.

B: I _____ as loud as I can. I _____
         (6)   (7)

to the airport to pick up a client. I'm late. Her plane _____
                                                              (8)

now, and I'm stuck[4] in traffic. I'm getting nervous. Cars aren't moving.

A: Why _____ moving?
            (9)

B: There's an accident on the highway.

A: I worry about you. _____?
                                          (10)

B: Of course, I'm wearing my seat belt.

A: That's good.

B: What _____ now?
                          (11)

A: I _____ the computer. I _____
            (12)   (13)

for information about cars on the Internet.

B: What _____ doing?
                          (14)

A: The kids? I can't hear you.

B: Yes, the kids.

A: Meg _____ TV. Pam _____ her
             (15)   (16)

homework.

B: Why _____ Meg doing her homework?
             (17)

A: She doesn't have any homework today.

B: _____ dinner for the kids?
          (18)

A: No, I'm not making dinner. I _____ for you to come
                                         (19)

home and make dinner.

B: Please don't wait for me. Oh. Traffic is finally moving. Talk to you
later.

---

[4] When you are stuck in traffic, you can't move because other cars aren't moving.

Before You Read

1. When you observe the students at this school, do you see any strange behaviors?

2. Is your behavior in this school different from your behavior when you are with your family or people from your native culture?

Read the following entry from Dan's journal. Pay special attention to verbs—simple present and present continuous.

October 8

I**'m sitting** in the school cafeteria now. I**'m writing** in my journal. I **want** to know about American customs, so I**'m observing** the behavior of other students. I **see** many strange behaviors and customs around me.

I**'m looking** at a young couple at the next table. The young man and woman **are touching, holding** hands, and even **kissing.** It looks strange because people never **kiss** in public in our country. At another table, a young man and woman **are sitting** with a baby. The man **is feeding** the baby. Men never **feed** the baby in our country. Why **isn't** the woman **feeding** the baby? Students in our country are usually single, not married with children.

Two women **are putting** on makeup. I **think** this is bad public behavior. These women **are wearing** shorts. In our country, women never **wear** shorts.

A group of students **is listening** to the radio. The music is very loud. Their music **is bothering** other people, but they **don't care.** I**'m sitting** far from them, but I **hear** their music.

A young man **is resting** his feet on another chair. His friend **is eating** a hamburger with his hands. Why **isn't** he **using** a fork and knife?

These kinds of behaviors **look** bad to me. I**'m trying** to understand them, but I**'m having** a hard time. I still **think** many of these actions are rude.[5]

---

[5]*Rude* means impolite.

6.5 | Contrast of Present Continuous and Simple Present

Form

Simple Present	Present Continuous
Dan sometimes **wears** a suit. He **doesn't** usually **wear** shorts. **Does** he ever **wear** a hat? Yes, he **does.** When **does** he **wear** a hat? Who **wears** a hat?	He **is wearing** jeans now. He **isn't wearing** a belt. **Is** he **wearing** a T-shirt? No, he **isn't.** What **is** he **wearing?** Who **is wearing** a T-shirt?

Uses

Examples	Explanation
a. Dan **writes** in his journal once a week in the college cafeteria. b. People **eat** hamburgers with their hands. c. The college cafeteria **has** inexpensive food.	We use the *simple present tense* to talk about: a. a habitual activity b. a custom c. a general truth or fact
a. Dan **is writing** in his journal now. b. He **is learning** more and more about life in the U.S.	We use the *present continuous tense* for: a. an action that is in progress at this moment b. a longer action that is in progress at this general time
Compare: Dan's family **lives** in another country. Dan **is living** in a dorm this semester.	When we use *live* in the simple present, we mean that this is a person's home. In the present continuous, it shows a temporary, short-term residence.
Compare: What **does** she **do** for a living? She's a nurse. What **is** she **doing?** She's waiting for the bus.	*What does she do?* asks about a profession or job. *What is she doing?* asks about her present activity.

EXERCISE 11 Two students meet in the cafeteria and discuss American customs and the customs of their native countries. Fill in the blanks with the correct form of the verb in parentheses ( ). Practice the simple present and the present continuous.

A: Hi. What _____ are you doing _____ here?
(example: you/do)

B: I _____ lunch. I always _____
(1 eat) (2 eat)

lunch at this time. But I _____ behaviors and
(3 also/observe)

customs in this country.

A: What do you mean?

B: Well, look at that man over there. He _____ an
(4 wear)

earring. It looks so strange. Only women _____
(5 wear)

earrings in my country.

A: It *is* strange. And look at that woman. She _____
(6 wear)

three earrings in one ear.

B: And she _____ running shoes with a dress. In my
(7 wear)

country, people only _____ running shoes for sports
(8 use)

activities.

A: Look at that student over there. He _____ a colored
(9 use)

pen to mark his textbook. In my country, we never _____
(10 write)

in our textbooks because they _____ to the college,
(11 belong)

not to the students.

B: Many college activities are different here. For example, my English

teacher usually _____ at the desk in class. In my
(12 sit)

country, the teacher always _____ in class. And the
(13 stand)

students always _____ when the teacher
(14 stand up)

_____ the room.
(15 enter)

A: And college students always _____ English or
(16 study)

another foreign language. Here, nobody knows another language.

My American roommate _____ five courses this
(17 take)

semester, but no foreign language.

B: By the way, how many classes _____ this semester?
(18 you/take)

The Present Continuous Tense   **171**

A: Four. In my country, I usually _____ eight courses a
(19 take)

semester, but my adviser here says I can only take four.

B: I have to go now. My girlfriend _____ for me at the
(20 wait)

library.

6.6 | Nonaction Verbs

Some verbs are nonaction verbs. Nonaction verbs describe a state or condition, not an action.

Examples	Explanation
He **hears** the music now. The music is bothering Dan, but the other students **don't care.** Dan **needs** a quiet place to write. He **doesn't understand** the behavior of some students. He **thinks** these behaviors are rude.	We do not usually use the present continuous tense with nonaction verbs. We use the *simple present tense,* even if we are talking about now.

Nonaction Verbs

like	know	see	cost
love	believe	smell	own
hate	think (that)	hear	have (for possession)
want	care (about)	taste	
need	understand	feel	
prefer	remember	seem	

Compare action and nonaction verbs.

Action (uses the present continuous tense)	Nonaction (uses the simple present tense)
The music **is bothering** Dan.	He **prefers** soft music.
Dan **is learning** about American customs.	He **cares** about good behavior.
He **is looking** at two people kissing.	This behavior **looks** strange to him.
He **is writing** about the students.	He **wants** to understand their customs.
He **is using** a laptop.	He **has** a PC in his dorm room.
The students **are listening** to the music.	Dan **hears** the music.
Dan **is looking** at students in the cafeteria.	He **sees** some strange behaviors.

Language Notes:
Hear and *see* are nonaction verbs. *Listen* and *look* are action verbs.
Hear and *see* are involuntary. *Listen* and *look* are voluntary.

EXERCISE 12   Fill in the blanks with the simple present or the present continuous tense of the verb in parentheses ( ).

EXAMPLES   I _____understand_____ the explanation now.
                      (understand)

I _____am writing_____ now.
              (write)

1. I _____ English this semester.
                      (study)

2. We _____ the textbook now.
                      (use)

3. We _____ a lot of practice with verb tenses.
                      (need)

4. We _____ action and nonaction verbs.
                      (compare)

5. I _____ every grammar rule.
                      (not/remember)

6. I _____ the chalkboard.
                      (see)

7. I _____ at the clock now. I _____
          (not/look)   *(look)*

   at my book.

8. I _____ my dictionary now.
                      (not/need)

9. We _____ a composition now.
                      (not/write)

10. We _____ the students in the next room.
                      (not/hear)

11. We _____ about nonaction verbs.
                      (learn)

12. We _____ a lot of grammar.
                      (know)

6.7 | *Think, Have,* and the Sense Perception Verbs

Think, have, and the sense perception verbs can be action or nonaction verbs.

Examples	Explanation
Action: He **is thinking** about his mother's cooking. **Nonaction:** He **thinks** it is wrong to kiss in public.	When we think <u>about</u> something, *think* is an action verb. When we *think* <u>that</u> something is true, *think* is a nonaction verb. We are giving an opinion about something.
Action: He **is having** lunch in the cafeteria. **Action:** He **is having** new experiences in the U.S. **Nonaction:** He **has** free time now. **Nonaction:** He **has** new American friends. **Nonaction:** His best friend **has** the flu now.	When *have* means to experience something or to eat or drink something, it is an action verb. When *have* shows possession, relationship, or illness, it is a nonaction verb.
Action: He **is looking** at a woman wearing shorts. **Nonaction:** This behavior **looks** bad to him. **Action:** He is **smelling** the coffee. **Nonaction:** The coffee **smells** delicious.	The sense perception verbs (*look, taste, feel, smell, sound, seem*) can be action or nonaction verbs. When the sense perception verbs describe a state, they are nonaction verbs. When they describe an action, they are action verbs.

EXERCISE **13** Fill in the blanks with the simple present or the present continuous tense of the verb in parentheses ( ).

EXAMPLES   I _____*am thinking*_____ about my family.

                (think)

I _____*think*_____ that life in the U.S. is not perfect.

    (think)

1. She _____ the flowers.

        (smell)

2. The flowers _____ beautiful.

          (smell)

3. They _____ about their children.

        (think)

4. They _____ that their children are wonderful.

        (think)

5. I _____ a good time in the U.S.

      (have)

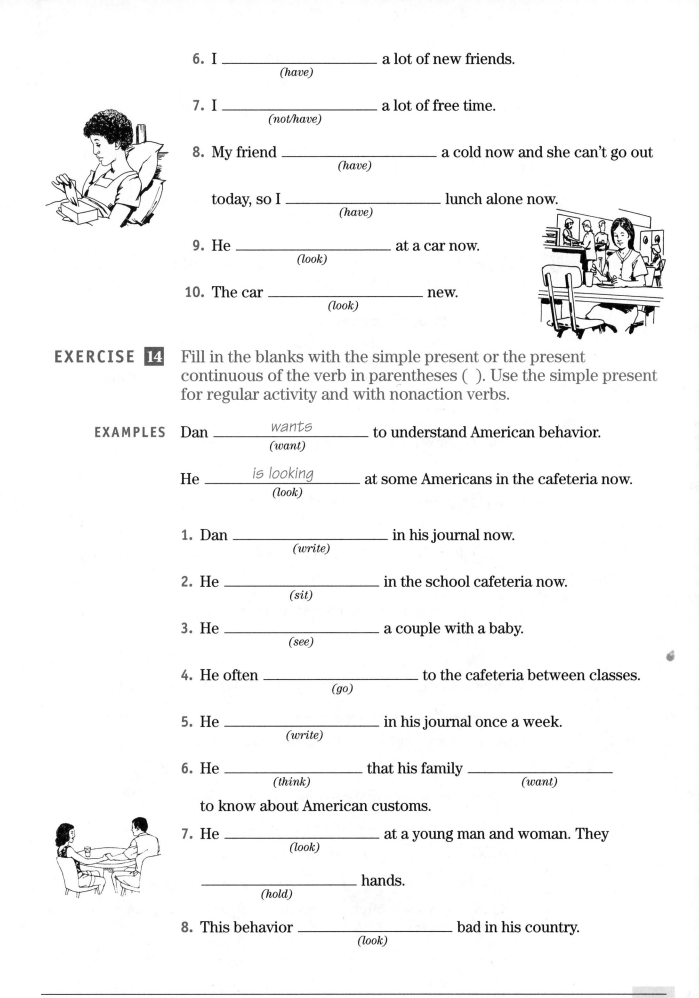

6. I _____ a lot of new friends.
   (have)

7. I _____ a lot of free time.
   (not/have)

8. My friend _____ a cold now and she can't go out
   (have)

   today, so I _____ lunch alone now.
   (have)

9. He _____ at a car now.
   (look)

10. The car _____ new.
    (look)

EXERCISE 14 Fill in the blanks with the simple present or the present continuous of the verb in parentheses ( ). Use the simple present for regular activity and with nonaction verbs.

EXAMPLES Dan _____ *wants* _____ to understand American behavior.
              (want)

              He _____ *is looking* _____ at some Americans in the cafeteria now.
              (look)

1. Dan _____ in his journal now.
   (write)

2. He _____ in the school cafeteria now.
   (sit)

3. He _____ a couple with a baby.
   (see)

4. He often _____ to the cafeteria between classes.
   (go)

5. He _____ in his journal once a week.
   (write)

6. He _____ that his family _____
   (think)   (want)

   to know about American customs.

7. He _____ at a young man and woman. They
   (look)

   _____ hands.
   (hold)

8. This behavior _____ bad in his country.
   (look)

9. He _____ about American customs now.
   (think)

10. Some women _____ shorts now.
    (wear)

11. Women in Dan's country never _____ shorts.
    (wear)

12. American customs _____ strange to him.
    (seem)

EXERCISE 15   Read each sentence. Write the negative form of the underlined word, using the word(s) in parentheses ( ).

EXAMPLES   Dan is looking at Americans. (people from his country)
He isn't looking at people from his country.

He knows about customs from his country. (American customs)
He doesn't know about American customs.

1. The father is feeding the baby. (the mother)

   _____

2. Dan's sitting in the cafeteria. (in class)

   _____

3. He understands customs from his country. (American customs)

   _____

4. American men and women sometimes kiss in public. (men and women in his country)

   _____

5. Americans use their hands to eat a hamburger. (to eat spaghetti)

   _____

6. A man is wearing an earring in one ear. (in both ears)

   _____

7. Americans seem strange to him. (to me)

   _____

8. American men like to take care of a baby. (Dan)

   _____

9. American women often wear shorts in the summer. (women in Dan's country never)

   _____

Read each sentence. Then write a *yes/no* question about the words in parentheses ( ). Write a short answer.

EXAMPLES   American women sometimes wear earrings. (American men/ever)
Do American men ever wear an earring? Yes, they do.

The women are wearing shorts. (the men)
Are the men wearing shorts? No, they aren't.

1. Dan is writing. (his homework)

_____

2. He's watching people. (American people)

_____

3. He understands his own customs. (American customs)

_____

4. American men wear shorts in the summer. (American women)

_____

5. The man is eating. (a hot dog)

_____

EXERCISE **17**   Read each statement. Then write a *wh-* question about the words in parentheses ( ). An answer is not necessary.

EXAMPLES   A young man is resting his feet on a chair. (why)
Why is he resting his feet on a chair?

Dan lives in the U.S. (where/his family)
Where does his family live?

1. Dan is writing a letter. (to whom) OR (who . . . to)

_____

2. Dan wants to know about American customs. (why)

_____

3. Two women are putting on makeup. (where)

_____

4. American men and women touch and hold hands in public. (why)

_____

5. Dan writes to his family. (how often)

_____

6. The man isn't using a fork. (why/not)

_____

7. Women don't wear shorts in some countries. (why)

_____

8. Americans often wear blue jeans. (why)

_____

9. "Custom" means tradition or habit. (what/"behavior")

_____

EXERCISE **18** *Combination exercise.* This is a phone conversation between Dan (D) and his mother (M). Fill in the blanks with the correct form of the words in parentheses ( ) to complete the conversation.

D: Hello?

M: Hi. This is Mom.

D: Hi, Mom. How _____*are you doing*_____?
(example: you/do)

M: We _____ fine. And you?
(1 do)

How _____ college in the U.S.?
(2 you/like)

D: Great. I _____ it a lot. I _____
(3 like)   (4 have)

a lot of fun.

M: Fun? _____?
(5 why/you/not/study)

D: I *am* studying. But I _____ new people from all over
(6 also/meet)

the world. I _____ about getting an earring.
(7 think)

M: What? Earrings are for women.

D: But, Mom, all the guys _____ it these days.
(8 do)

M: I _____. You _____ an earring in your
(9 not/care)   (10 not/need)

ear. You just _____ to study. _____
(11 need)   (12 you/get)

good grades?

D: You _____ I'm a good student. Of course,
(13 know)

I _____ good grades.
(14 get)

M: _____ your guitar these days?
(15 you/practice)

D: Yes, I am. But I _____ as much time as before.
(16 not/have)

I _____ five classes this semester.
(17 take)

M: Only five? Students here _____ eight classes.
(18 usually/take)

D: The system is different here. Freshmen only take four or five classes.

M: What _____?
(19 freshman/mean)

D: A freshman is a student in the first year of college.

M: How's the food? _____ enough to eat?
(20 you/get)

D: Yes, I am. In fact, I _____ weight. But I
(21 gain)

_____ the food here.
(22 not/like)

M: Why _____ the food?
(23 not/like)

D: It's too greasy. And it _____ like food back home.
(24 not/taste)

I really _____ your food.
(25 miss)

M: I _____ your favorite dish now.
(26 make)

D: Really? I _____ hungry just thinking about it.
(27 get)

M: You and Dad _____ that my food is the best.
(28 always/think)

D: Where's Dad?

M: He _____ in the garden now. He's planting a new tree.
(29 work)

D: Thanks for sending me the sweater. I _____ it now.
(30 wear)

M: _____ enough warm clothes?
(31 you/have)

D: For now, I do. But it _____ to get cold these days.
(32 start)

And the days _____ shorter. Fall is beautiful here.
(33 get)

The trees _____ color. I _____
(34 change)   (35 look)

out my window now and I _____ a beautiful maple
(36 see)

tree with red leaves. But I _____ the climate back
(37 prefer)

home. It's warm all year. Here it's really cold in December and January.

M: I _____ a new sweater for you now. Your sister Ruby
(38 make)

_____ you a scarf.
(39 make)

D: Thanks, Mom. Where's Ruby? _____ to talk to me now?
(40 she/want)

M: I _____ so. She _____ a video
(41 not/think)   (42 watch)

with her friends.

D: _____ good grades this semester?
(43 she/get)

M: She _____ too much time with her friends these days.
(44 spend)

D: Well, she's 16. Friends are really important when you're 16.
M: I'm worried about her.
D: Don't worry so much, Mom.

M: Of course I worry. I'm a mother. Dad _____ in now.
(45 come)

He _____ to talk to you now.
(46 want)

D: OK, Mom. Bye.

Uses of Tenses

Simple Present Tense	
General truths	Americans **speak** English. Oranges **grow** in Florida.
Regular activity, habit	I always **speak** English in class. I sometimes **eat** in the cafeteria. I **visit** my parents every Friday.
Customs	Americans **shake** hands. Japanese people **bow.**
Place of origin	Miguel **comes** from El Salvador. Marek **comes** from Poland.
With nonaction verbs	She **has** a new car. I **like** the U.S. You **look** great today.

Present Continuous (with action verbs only)	
Now	We **are reviewing** now. I **am looking** at page 181 now.
A long action in progress at this general time	Dan **is learning** about American customs. He **is studying** English.
A descriptive state	She **is wearing** shorts. He **is sitting** near the door. The teacher **is standing.**

1. Include *be* with a continuous tense.

   is
   He working now.
   ^

2. Use the correct word order in a question.

   are you
   Where ~~you're~~ going?

   don't you
   Why ~~you don't~~ like New York?

3. Don't use the present continuous with a nonaction verb.

   has
   She ~~is having~~ her own computer.

4. Use the *-s* form when the subject is *he*, *she*, or *it*.

   has   *s*
   He ~~have~~ a new car. He like to drive.
                              ^

5. Don't use *be* with a simple present-tense verb.

   ~~I'm~~ need a new computer.

6. Use *do* or *does* in a simple present-tense question.

   does   *live*
   Where ~~lives~~ your mother ?
                          ^

7. Don't use the *-s* form after *does*.

   Where does he ~~takes~~ the bus?

Review the Editing Advice for the simple present tense on pages 68–69.

PART 1 Find the mistakes with the underlined words and correct them. Not every sentence has a mistake. If the sentence is correct, write *C*.

EXAMPLES   She's ~~owning~~ a new bike now. *owns*
I'm not studying math this semester.   *C*

1. Why you aren't listening to me?

2. Usually I'm go home after class.

3. I think that he's having trouble with this lesson.

4. She's thinking about her family now.

5. Does she needs help with her homework?

6. What kind of car do you have?

7. What he's studying now?

8. Does he has any children?

9. He's wearing jeans now.

10. My teacher speak English well.

11. I'm speak my native language at home.

12. The baby sleeping now.

13. When begins summer?

14. Where does your family lives?

PART 2 This is a conversation between two students, Alicia (A) and Teresa (T), who meet in the school library. Fill in the blanks with the simple present or the present continuous form of the verb in parentheses ( ).

T: Hi, Alicia.

A: Hi, Teresa. What _____ *are you doing* _____ here?
(example: you/do)

T: I _____ for a book on American geography. What
(1 look)

about you?

A: I _____ a book. _____ to go for
(2 return)   *(3 you/want)*

a cup of coffee?

The Present Continuous Tense   **183**

T: I can't. I _____ for my friend. We _____
(4 wait)   (5 work)

on a geography project together, and we _____ to
(6 need)

finish it by next week.

A: _____ your geography class?
(7 you/like)

T: Yes. I especially _____ the teacher, Bob. He's a
(8 like)

handsome young man. He's very casual. He always

_____ jeans and a T-shirt to class. He
(9 wear)

_____ an earring in one ear.
(10 have)

A: That _____ very strange to me.
(11 seem)

I _____ that teachers in the U.S. are very informal.
(12 think)

How _____ the class? By lecturing?
(13 Bob/teach)

T: No. We _____ in small groups, and he
(14 usually/work)

_____ us by walking around the classroom.
(15 help)

A: _____ hard tests?
(16 he/give)

T: No. He _____ in tests.
(17 not/believe)

A: Why _____ in tests?
(18 he/not/believe)

T: He _____ that students get too nervous during a test.
(19 think)

He _____ it's better to work on projects. This week
(20 say)

we _____ on city maps.
(21 work)

A: That _____ interesting.
(22 sound)

T: Why _____ me so many questions about my teacher?
(23 you/ask)

A: I _____ about taking a geography course next
(24 think)

semester.

T: Bob's very popular. Be sure to register early because his classes

always _____ quickly. Oh. I _____
(25 fill) _(26 see)_

my friend now. She _____ toward us. I have to go now.
(27 walk)

A: Good luck on your project.

T: Thanks. Bye.

PART 3 Fill in the blanks with the negative form of the underlined word.

EXAMPLE   Teresa <u>is</u> in the library. She _____<u>isn't</u>_____ at home.

1. Alicia <u>wants</u> to go for a cup of coffee. Teresa _____ to
go for a cup of coffee.

2. Teresa <u>is looking</u> for a book. Alicia _____ for a book.

3. They <u>are talking</u> about school. They _____ about the
news.

4. They <u>have</u> time to talk now. They _____ time for a cup
of coffee.

5. Students in the geography class <u>work</u> in small groups.

They _____ alone.

6. Alicia's teacher <u>gives</u> tests. Teresa's teacher _____ tests.

7. Teresa <u>is waiting</u> for a friend. Alicia _____ for a friend.

8. The teacher <u>seems</u> strange to Alicia. He _____ strange
to Teresa.

9. Alicia <u>is returning</u> a book. Teresa _____ a book.

PART 4 Read each sentence. Then write a _yes/no_ question about the
words in parentheses ( ). Write a short answer.

EXAMPLE   Teresa is looking for a book. (a geography book)
Is she looking for a geography book? Yes, she is.

1. Bob likes projects. (tests)

_____

2. Alicia has time now. (Teresa)

_____

3. They are talking about their classes. (their teachers)

_____

4. Bob wears jeans to class. (ever / a suit)

_____

5. Alicia wants to go for coffee. (Teresa)

_____

6. American teachers seem strange to Alicia. (to Teresa)

_____

7. Teresa is working on a geography project. (Alicia)

_____

PART 5 Read each sentence. Then write a question with the words in parentheses ( ). An answer is not necessary.

EXAMPLE Bob is popular. (Why)
Why is he popular? _____

1. Bob sounds interesting. (Why)

_____

2. Bob doesn't like tests. (Why)

_____

3. Teresa and her friend are working on a project. (What kind of project)

_____

4. Teresa studies in the library. (How often)

_____

5. Teresa is looking for a book. (What kind)

_____

6. Teresa is waiting for her friend. (Why)

_____

7. Her classmates aren't writing a term paper. (Why)

_____

Classroom Activities

1. Think of a place (cafeteria, airport, train station, bus, playground, church, opera, movie theater, laundry, office at this school, kindergarten classroom, restaurant, department store, etc.). Pretend you are at this place. Write three or four sentences to tell what people in this place are doing. Other students will guess where you are.

   EXAMPLE   People are walking fast.
   People are carrying suitcases.
   People are standing in long lines.
   They're buying tickets.
   Guess: Are you at the airport?

2. Pretend you are calling from your cell phone. You are telling your family where you are. Fill in the blanks to tell what you and other people are doing. Then find a partner and see how many of your sentences match your partner's sentences.

   a. I'm at the supermarket. I'm _____.
   Do you need anything while I'm here?

   b. I'm in my car. I'm _____.

   c. I'm in the school library. I'm _____.

   People _____ me to be quiet because

   I'm _____ to you on my cell phone.

   d. I'm in a taxi. I'm on my way home. I'm _____

   you to let you know that _____.

   e. I'm at the bus stop. I _____ for the bus,
   but it's late. I don't want you to worry.

   f. I'm at a shoe store. I _____.

   g. I'm at the playground with the kids. The kids _____

   _____.

   h. I'm at the movies. I can't talk now because the movie _____

   _____.

   i. I'm in the bedroom. I have to talk softly because my roommate

   _____.

   j. I'm in class now. I can't talk. The teacher _____

   _____.

3. In a small group or with the entire class, discuss behaviors that are strange to you. What American behaviors are not polite in your native culture?

Outside Activity

Go to the school cafeteria, student union, or other crowded place. Sit there for a while and look for unusual behaviors. Write down some of the unusual things you see. Report back to the class.

Internet Activity

Find the Web site of a college in this city. Answer the following questions:

1. Where is it?

2. What's the tuition?

3. Does this college have evening classes?

4. Does this college have more than one location?

5. Does it have a graduate program?

6. Does it have dormitories?

7. Does it have ESL classes?

8. When is the next registration?

9. What are the vacation days?

 Additional Activities at **http://elt.thomson.com/gic**

LESSON

7

GRAMMAR

Future Tenses—*Will* and *Be Going To*
Comparison of Tenses

CONTEXT: Weddings

Planning for a Wedding
Jason and Katie—Starting a Married Life

PLANNING FOR A WEDDING

1. In your native culture, what kind of gifts do people give to a bride and groom?

2. Are weddings expensive in your native culture?

Read the following article. Pay special attention to future-tense verbs.

Karyn and Steve are engaged now and are planning their wedding. They need a lot of time to plan. They**'re going to graduate** from college next year, and the wedding **will take** place a year and a half after they graduate from college. They **will need** time to choose a photographer, invitations, a place for the reception,[1] a wedding dress, flowers, rings, a wedding cake, entertainment, and more. The wedding **is going to be** very expensive. In addition to paying for the wedding and reception, they **will need** to rent a limousine and pay for a rehearsal dinner and a honeymoon. They **are going to invite** about 250 people, including many friends and relatives from out of town. They **are going to pay** for the hotel rooms for their grandparents, aunts, and uncles. It **is going to take** a lot of time and energy to plan for the wedding.

Before their wedding, they **will register** for gifts. They **will go** to stores and select the gifts they want to receive. When guests go to the stores, they **will choose** a gift from this list. This way, Karyn and Steve **are going to receive** exactly what they want. They **won't receive** duplicate presents. About six or seven weeks before the wedding, they **will send** out their invitations. After they return from their honeymoon in Hawaii, they **are going to send** thank-you cards to all the guests.

Who**'s going to pay** for all this? After they graduate, they **will work** and **save** money for their dream wedding. But their parents **are going to help** too. Like many young couples, they **will have** credit card debt for years after the wedding. This is in addition to college debt.

[1] A *reception* is a party after a wedding.

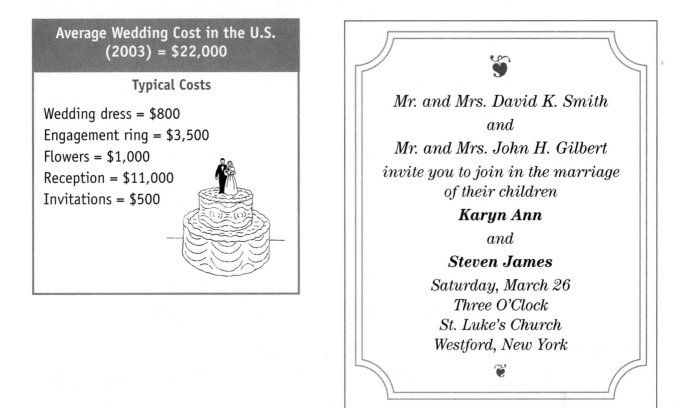

Average Wedding Cost in the U.S. (2003) = $22,000

Typical Costs

Wedding dress = $800
Engagement ring = $3,500
Flowers = $1,000
Reception = $11,000
Invitations = $500

Mr. and Mrs. David K. Smith
and
Mr. and Mrs. John H. Gilbert
invite you to join in the marriage
of their children
Karyn Ann
and
Steven James
Saturday, March 26
Three O'Clock
St. Luke's Church
Westford, New York

7.1 | Future with *Will*

Examples	Explanation
Subject *Will* **Verb** **Complement** They **will** **rent** a limousine. There **will** **be** a reception. The bride **will** **wear** a white dress.	We use *will* + the base form for the future tense. *Will* doesn't have an *-s* form.

They'll register for gifts.
She'll buy a white dress.
He'll rent a tuxedo.
It'll take them a long time to plan for the wedding.
	We can make a contraction with the subject pronoun and *will*.
	  I will = I'll It will = It'll
	  You will = You'll We will = We'll
	  He will = He'll They will = They'll
	  She will = She'll

They **will not receive** duplicate presents. They **won't pay** for everything. Their parents will help them.	Put *not* after *will* to form the negative. The contraction for *will not* is *won't*.
I will **always** love you. I will **never** leave you. We will **probably** give money as a gift.	You can put an adverb (*always, never, probably, even*) between *will* and the main verb.

EXERCISE 1 Fill in the blanks with an appropriate verb in the future tense. Practice *will*.

EXAMPLE Karyn and Steve's wedding _____*will be*_____ in a church.

1. They _____ 250 guests.

2. The wedding _____ expensive.

3. They _____ to Hawaii on their honeymoon.

4. They _____ debt for many years after the wedding.

5. Guests _____ presents that the bride and groom want.

6. The bride and groom _____ a limousine.

7. Their parents _____ them pay for the wedding.

7.2 | Future with *Be Going To*

Examples					Explanation
Subject	**Be**	**Going To**	**Verb**	**Complement**	Use *is/am/are* + *going to* + the base form for the future tense.
I	**am**	**going to**	**buy**	a gift.	We can make a contraction with the subject pronoun and *is, am, are:*
You	**are**	**going to**	**attend**	the wedding.	**I'm** going to buy a gift.
They	**are**	**going to**	**send**	invitations.	We can make a contraction with a singular noun + *is:*
The bride	**is**	**going to**	**wear**	a white dress.	The **bride's** going to wear a white dress.

Examples	Explanation
They **are not going to graduate** this year. Their parents **aren't going to pay** for everything.	To make a negative statement, put *not* after *is/am/are.*
They **are going to go** on a honeymoon. OR They **are going** on a honeymoon.	When the main verb is *to go,* we often delete it.
They **are probably going** to open their gifts at home. They **are always going** to remember their wedding day.	We can put an adverb (*always, never, probably, even*) between *is, am, are* and *going.*

Pronunciation Notes:

1. In informal speech, *going to* before another verb often sounds like "gonna." We don't write "gonna."

2. We only pronounce "gonna" before a verb. We don't pronounce "gonna" in the following sentence: They are going to Hawaii.

Listen to your teacher pronounce the sentences in the above boxes.

EXERCISE 2 Fill in the blanks with an appropriate verb in the future tense.
Practice *be going to*.

EXAMPLE They ___are going to send___ thank-you cards to the guests.

1. Musicians _____ at the wedding.

2. A professional photographer _____ pictures.

3. There _____ a lot of people at the wedding.

4. The bride _____ a white dress.

5. The wedding _____ a lot of money.

6. They _____ wedding debt and college debt for many years.

7. The wedding cake _____ very expensive.

7.3 | Choosing *Will* or *Be Going To*

Examples	Explanation
I think the newlyweds **will** be very happy together. I think the newlyweds **are going to** be very happy together.	For a prediction, we can use either *will* or *be going to*.
The wedding **will** be in a church. The wedding **is going to** be in a church. They **will** send out 250 invitations. They **are going to** send out 250 invitations.	For a simple fact about the future, we can use either *will* or *be going to*.
I **will** always love you. I **will** never leave you.	For a promise, use *will*.
A: What gift are you planning to give your cousin for the wedding? B: I don't know. Maybe I'**ll** just give money.	Use *will* when you don't have a previous plan, but you decide what to do at the time of speaking.
A: This gift box is heavy. B: I'**ll** carry it for you.	When you offer to help someone, use *will*.
They **are going to** get married on May 6. I **am going to** buy a gift. Guests **are going to** come from out of town.	When we have a previous plan to do something, we usually use *be going to*. *I'm **going** to buy a gift.* = *I'm **planning** to buy a gift.*

EXERCISE **3** ABOUT YOU Tell if you have plans to do these things or not. Use *be going to*.

EXAMPLE meet a friend after class.
I'm (not) going to meet a friend after class.

1. get something to eat after class
2. watch TV tonight
3. eat dinner at home tonight
4. go to the library this week
5. go shopping for groceries this week
6. stay home this weekend
7. take a vacation this year
8. move (to a different apartment) this year
9. buy a car this year

EXERCISE **4** ABOUT YOU Tell if you predict that these things are going to happen or not in this class. Use *be going to*.

EXAMPLE we / finish this lesson today
We are going to finish this lesson today.

1. the teacher / give a test soon
2. the test / be hard
3. most students / pass the test
4. I / pass the test
5. the teacher / give everyone an A
6. my English / improve
7. we / finish this book by the end of the semester
8. the next test / cover the future tense
9. we / have a party at the end of the semester

EXERCISE **5** Fill in the blanks to complete these statements. Use *be going to*.

EXAMPLE I don't understand the meaning of a word. _I'm going to look it up in_ my dictionary.

1. It's hot in here. I _____ a window.

2. It's too noisy in this house. I can't study. I _____ the library.

3. She's hungry. She _____ dinner now.

4. My mother in Poland always worries about me. I _____

_____ to tell her that I'm fine.

5. We don't have any milk in the house. When I go out shopping, I

_____ some milk.

6. She plans to be a doctor. She _____ medical school next year.

7. I'm not happy with my job. I _____ and look for another one.

8. I _____ next week. Here's my new address.

9. My parents miss me very much. They _____ next month to visit for three weeks.

10. There's a great new movie at the Garden Theater. My friends and

I _____ tomorrow night. Do you want to go with us?

EXERCISE **6** Tell if you predict that these things will happen or not in the next 50 years. Use *will*. You may work with a partner or in a small group.

EXAMPLE people / have more free time
I think people won't have more free time. They will spend more time at their jobs and less time with their families.

1. there / another world war

2. the economy of the U.S. / get worse

3. people in the U.S. / have fewer children

4. Americans / live longer

5. health care / improve

   6. cars / use solar energy[2]

   7. divorce / increase

   8. crime / get worse

   9. people / get tired of computers

   10. technology / continue to grow

EXERCISE 7 Some friends of yours are going to have a birthday soon, and you want to buy them a present or do something special for them. What will you buy or do for these people?

EXAMPLE Maria's birthday is in the winter.
I'll buy her a sweater.   OR   I'll take her skiing.

   1. Bill loves to go fishing.

   2. Tina loves to eat in restaurants.

   3. Carl needs a new radio.

   4. Jim has a new CD player.

   5. Lisa loves the beach in the summer.

   6. Tom loves movies.

EXERCISE 8 A man is proposing marriage to a woman. He is making promises. Fill in the blanks to complete these statements.

EXAMPLE I _____*will be*_____ a good husband to you.

   1. I love you very much. I (always) _____ you.

   2. I want to make you happy. I _____ everything I can to make you happy.

   3. I don't have a lot of money, but I _____ and try to make money.

   4. We _____ children, and I _____ a good father to them.

   5. We _____ old together.

   6. We _____ best friends and take care of each other.

   7. You are the only woman for me. I (not) _____ at another woman.

   [2]*Solar energy* comes from the sun.

EXERCISE 9 Offer to help in these situations using *will* + an appropriate verb.

EXAMPLE A: I have to move next Sunday. It's so much work.

B: *Don't worry. I'll help you pack.*

1. A: My hands are full. I need to open the door.

   B: _____

2. A: I need stamps, but I have no time to go to the post office.

   B: I'm going to the post office. _____

3. A: I cook every night. I'm tired of cooking.

   B: Take a break. _____ tonight.

4. A: I don't have experience with computers. I have to write my composition on the computer.

   B: Come to my house after class. _____

5. A: I always drive when we go to the country. I'm tired.

   B: No problem. _____ this time.

6. A: Let's go out to dinner tonight.

   B: I can't. I don't have any money.

   A: That's okay. _____

7. A: I can't pay my phone bill. I'm not working now and don't have much money.

   B: Don't worry. _____. You can pay me back next month.

8. A: The phone's ringing and I'm eating a sandwich. My mouth is full.

   B: Finish your lunch. _____

7.4 | Questions with *Be Going To*

Compare Affirmative Questions and Statements

Wh-Word	Be	Subject	Be	Going To + Base Form	Complement	Short Answer
		You	are	going to send	a gift.	
	Are	you		going to send	money?	No, I'm not.
What	are	you		going to send?		Towels.
		Who	is	going to send	money?	Her uncle is.
		She	is	going to wear	a white dress.	
	Is	she		going to wear	white shoes?	Yes, she is.
		Who	is	going to wear	a tuxedo?	The groom is.

Compare Negative Questions and Statements

Wh-Word	Be + n't	Subject	Be + n't	Going To + Base Form	Complement
		You	aren't	going to attend	the wedding.
Why	aren't	you		going to attend?	

EXERCISE 10 ABOUT YOU Ask another student a *yes/no* question with *are you going to* about a time later today. Then ask a *wh-* question with the words in parentheses ( ) whenever possible.

EXAMPLE listen to the radio (when)

A: Are you going to listen to the radio tonight?
B: Yes, I am.

A: When are you going to listen to the radio?
B: After dinner.

1. watch TV (what show)

2. listen to the radio (when)

3. read the newspaper (what newspaper)

4. go shopping (why)

5. take a shower (when)

6. eat dinner (with whom) OR (who . . . with)

7. call someone (whom)

8. check your e-mail (when)

9. do your homework (when)

EXERCISE ⑪ Ask another student a *yes/no* question with *be going to* and the words given. Then ask a *wh-* question with the words in parentheses ( ) whenever possible.

EXAMPLE study another English course after this one (which course)

A: Are you going to study another English course after this one?
B: Yes, I am.

A: Which course are you going to study?
B: I'm going to study level 4.

1. stay in this city (why)

2. study something new (what)

3. look for a job (when)

4. get an A in this course (what grade)

5. buy a computer (why) (what kind)

6. visit other American cities (which cities)

7. transfer to another school (why) (which school)

7.5 | Questions with *Will*

Compare Affirmative Questions and Statements						
Wh-Word	**Will**	**Subject**	**Will**	**Base Form**	**Complement**	**Short Answer**
		The wedding	will	begin	soon.	
	Will	the wedding		begin	in 15 minutes?	Yes, it will.
When	will	the wedding		begin?		At 8 o'clock.
		Who	will	begin	the wedding?	The groom will.

Compare Negative Questions and Statements					
Wh-Word	**Won't**	**Subject**	**Won't**	**Base Form**	**Complement**
		The groom	won't	pay	for the whole wedding.
Why	won't	the groom		pay	for the whole wedding?

EXERCISE 12 Fill in the blanks with the correct form of the verb in ( ).
Use *will* for the future.

1. **A:** I don't have time to shop for a wedding gift, and the wedding is tomorrow.

   B: What _____*will you do*_____?
   (example: you/do)

   A: I _____ a check.
   (probably/send)

2. **A:** What time _____?
   (the wedding/start)

   B: The invitation says it _____ at 5:30 p.m., but
   (start)

   usually weddings don't start exactly on time.

3. **A:** Where _____?
   (the wedding/be)

   B: It'll be in a hotel.

4. **A:** What _____ to the wedding?
   (you/wear)

   B: I don't know. I _____ my blue suit. Oh. I just
   (probably/wear)

   remembered my blue suit is dirty. I _____ time
   (not/have)

   to take it to the cleaners. I _____ wear my gray suit.
   (have to)

5. **A:** How many people _____ the wedding?
   (attend)

   B: About 200 people _____ the wedding.
   (attend)

6. **A:** What kind of food _____ at the reception?
   (they/serve)

   B: There _____ a choice of chicken or fish.
   (be)

7. **A:** Do you think the bride and groom _____ happy
   (be)

   together?

   B: Yes, I think they _____. They love each other
   (be)

   very much.

8. **A:** I'm going to a store to check the wedding registry.

 B: I _____ with you.
 (go)

 A: It's late. The store _____ closed by the time we
 (probably/ be)

 arrive. I _____ tomorrow morning instead.
 (go)

9. **A:** How long _____?
 (the wedding/last)

 B: The ceremony _____ about a half hour. Then
 (probably/last)

 there's a dinner. People _____ for hours after
 (probably/stay)

 the dinner to dance.

10. **A:** _____ for their
 (the bride and groom/leave)

 honeymoon immediately?

 B: Probably not. They _____ tired after the
 (be)

 wedding. They _____ the next day.
 (probably/leave)

EXERCISE 13 In this conversation, fill in the blanks using the words in
parentheses ( ). Choose *will* or *be going to* for the future tenses.
In some cases, both answers are possible.

 A: I'm so excited. My sister ____is going to get____ married
 (example: get)

 next year.

 B: Why are *you* so excited?

 A: I'm going to be a bridesmaid.

 B: How many bridesmaids _____?
 (1 she/have)

 A: Three.

 B: What kind of dresses _____ ?
 (2 the bridesmaids/wear)

 A: All the bridesmaids _____ blue dresses,
 (3 wear)

 but each one _____ her own style.
 (4 choose)

 B: _____ in your church?
 (5 the wedding/be)

A: No, it isn't. It's going to be outdoors, in a garden. After that, there

_____ a dinner at a restaurant.
        (6 be)

B: Why _____ to get married?
                    (7 they/wait)

A: They're both in college now, and they want to get married after they finish college.

B: Where _____ after they get married?
                    (8 live)

A: Probably here for a while. But then they _____
                                                    (9 look)

for jobs in the Boston area.

B: How many people _____ to the wedding?
                            (10 invite)

A: It _____ a big wedding because we have a large
            (11 be)

family, and so does her boyfriend, Joe. They _____
                                                    (12 invite)

about 400 people.

B: Wow! The wedding _____ expensive.
                            (13 be)

Who _____ for it?
                    (14 pay)

A: Our parents and Joe's parents _____. They

_____ the cost 50/50. A lot of relatives
        (15 split)

and friends _____ here from out of town.
                    (16 come)

B: Where _____?
                    (17 they/stay)

A: In hotels.

B: It's _____ expensive for the guests too. They
                (18 be)

_____ pay for their flights,
                (19 have to)

hotels, and a wedding gift.

A: I know. But they want to come. Of course, some people

_____ because it _____ too
        (20 not come)   *(21 be)*

expensive for them.

7.6 | Future Tense + Time/*If* Clause[3]

Time or *If* Clause (Simple Present Tense)	Main Clause (Future Tense)	Explanation
After they **graduate,**	they **are going to work.**	The sentences on the left have two clauses, a time or *if* clause and a main clause.
Before they **get** married,	they **are going to send** out invitations.	
When they **return** from the honeymoon,	they **will send** thank-you cards.	We use the *future* only in the main clause; we use the *simple present tense* in the time/*if* clause.
If their grandparents **come** from out of town,	they **will pay** for their hotel.	

Main Clause (Future Tense)	Time or *If* Clause (Simple Present Tense)	Explanation
They **are going to work**	after they **graduate.**	We can put the main clause before the time/*if* clause.
Their grandparents **will stay** in a hotel	if they **come.**	

Punctuation Note:
If the time/*if* clause comes before the main clause, we use a comma to separate the two parts of the sentence. If the main clause comes first, we don't use a comma.

Compare:

> If I get an invitation, I'll go to the wedding.
> I'll go to the wedding if I get an invitation.

Usage Note:
There is a proverb that means "I will decide when I need to decide." The proverb is:

> *I'll cross that bridge when I get to it.*

---

[3] A clause is a group of words that has a subject and a verb. Some sentences have more than one clause.

EXERCISE 14 This is an old fable.[4] It's the story of a young lady. She is carrying a pail of milk to the market. As she walks there, she thinks about what she will do with the money that the milk will bring. Fill in the blanks with the correct form of the verb to complete this story.

EXAMPLE When I _____*sell*_____ this milk, I _____*will buy*_____ some eggs.
                       (sell)   (buy)

1. When the eggs _____, I _____
                      (hatch)   (have)
   many chickens.

2. I _____ the chickens when they _____
        (sell)   (be)
   big.

3. When I _____ the chickens, I _____
              (sell)   (have)
   money to buy a pretty new dress.

4. I _____ to a party when I _____
        (go)   (have)
   my new dress.

5. All the young men _____ me when I
                          (notice)

   _____ the dress.
          (wear)

6. When the men _____ how pretty I am, they
                       (see)

   _____ to marry me.
          (want)

Suddenly the young woman drops the milk pail and all the milk spills.

What lesson does this story try to teach us?

EXERCISE 15 ABOUT YOU Complete each statement.

EXAMPLES When this class is over, _____*I'll go home.*_____

When this class is over, _____*I'm going to get something to eat.*_____

1. When this semester is over, _____

2. When this class is over, _____

3. When I get home today, _____

4. When I graduate (or finish my courses at this school), _____

_____

---

[4] A *fable* is an old story. It usually teaches us a lesson, called a moral.

5. When I return to my country / become a citizen, _____

6. When I retire, _____

7. When I speak English better, _____

EXERCISE 16   ABOUT YOU Complete each statement.

EXAMPLES   If I drink too much coffee, _____ *I won't sleep tonight.* _____

If I drink too much coffee, _____ *I'm going to feel nervous.* _____

1. If I practice English, _____

2. If I don't study, _____

3. If I don't pay my rent, _____

4. If I pass this course, _____

5. If we have a test next week, _____

6. If the teacher is absent tomorrow, _____

7. If I find a good job, _____

EXERCISE 17   On the first day of class, a teacher is explaining the course to the students. Fill in the blanks to complete this conversation between a teacher (T) and her students (S).

T: In this course, you _____ *are going to study* _____ English grammar. You
                                                              (example: study)

_____ a few short compositions. Tomorrow,
                (1 write)

I _____ you a list of assignments. Do you
                (2 give)

have any questions about this course?

S: Yes. How many tests _____?
                                     (3 have)

T: You will have 14 tests, one for each lesson in the book. If you're

absent from a test, you can make it up.[5] If you _____
                                                     (4 not take)

the test, you _____ an F on that test.
                       (5 get)

S: _____ us about the tests ahead of time?
                   (6 tell)

T: Oh, yes. I'll always tell you about a test a few days before.

---

[5] If you are absent on the day of a test, the teacher expects you to take it at a later time.

S: When _____ the midterm exam?
(7 give)

T: I'm going to give you the midterm exam in April.

S: _____ very hard?
(8 be)

T: If you _____, it won't be hard.
(9 study)

S: What _____ in this course?
(10 study)

T: You'll study verb tenses, count and noncount nouns, and comparison of adjectives.

S: _____ everything in this book?
(11 finish)

T: Yes, I think we'll finish everything.

S: _____ over?
(12 be)

T: The semester will be over[6] in June. Tomorrow I _____
(13 give)
you a course outline with all this information.

EXERCISE 18 Write two questions to ask your teacher about this course.

EXAMPLES *Will there be a test on this lesson?*

When will you give us the next test?

_____

_____

EXERCISE 19 A young woman (A) is going to leave her country to go to the U.S. Her friend (B) is asking her questions. Fill in the blanks to complete this conversation.

A: I'm so happy! I'm going to the U.S.

B: When *are you going to leave?*
(example: leave)

A: I'm going to leave next month.

B: So soon? _____ anything
(1 buy)
before you _____?
(2 leave)

---

[6] To *be over* means to be finished.

A: Yes. I'm going to buy warm clothes for the winter. I hear the winter there is very cold.

B: Where _____?

(3 be)

A: I'll be in Ann Arbor, Michigan.

Ann Arbor, Michigan

B: Where _____?

(4 live)

A: I'm not sure. When I _____ there,

(5 get)

I _____ where to live.

(6 decide)

B: _____ in the U.S.?

(7 work)

A: No, I'm not going to work. I have a scholarship. I'm going to study at the University of Michigan.

B: What _____?

(8 study)

A: I'm going to study to be a computer analyst.

B: When _____ to our country?

(9 return)

A: I _____ when I _____.

(10 return)   (11 graduate)

B: When _____?

(12 you/graduate)

A: In four years.

B: That's a long time! _____ me?

(13 miss)

A: Of course, I'll miss you.

B: _____ to me?

(14 write)

A: Of course. I _____ to you when I _____

(15 write)   (16 find)

a place to live.

EXERCISE 20

A young Korean woman and her fiancé, Kim, are planning to get married. Her friend is asking her questions about her plans. Fill in the blanks to complete this conversation.

A: I'm getting married!

B: That's wonderful! Congratulations. ___*Are you going to have*___ a big
(example: have)

wedding?

A: No, we're going to have a small wedding. We _____
(1 invite)

about 50 people.

B: Where _____?
(2 be)

A: It'll be at St. Peter's Church. We _____ a reception
(3 have)

at a Korean restaurant after the wedding.

B: _____ a wedding dress?
(4 buy)

A: No, I _____ my sister's dress for the
(5 use)

wedding. Then, for the reception, I _____
(6 wear)

a traditional Korean dress.

B: Where _____ after you get married?
(7 live)

A: For a few years, we _____ with Kim's
(8 live)

parents. When Kim _____ college and
(9 finish)

_____ a job, we _____
(10 get)   (11 get)

our own apartment.

B: You're going to live with your in-laws? I can't believe it.

A: In my country, it's common. My in-laws are very nice.

I'm sure it _____ a problem.
(12 not/be)

We _____ children right away.
(13 not/have)

B: _____ here for the wedding?
(14 come)

A: No, my parents aren't going to come. But a month after the wedding,

we _____ a trip to Korea,
(15 take)

and Kim can meet my parents there.

B: _____ married?
        (16 get)

A: On May 15. I hope you'll be able to attend. We _____
                                                        (17 send)

you an invitation.

B: I _____ glad to attend.
           (18 be)

JASON AND KATIE—STARTING A MARRIED LIFE

Before You Read

1. Do you think life is hard for newlyweds? In what way?

2. In your community, do parents help their children after they get married?

Read the following article. Pay special attention to verb tenses: simple present, present continuous, and future.

Jason and Katie are newlyweds. The wedding is over, the honeymoon was great, the gifts are opened, and their life as a married couple **is beginning.** They **are learning** that they have many responsibilities as a married couple.

Katie **works** as a nurse full-time. She **doesn't work** in a hospital. She **goes** to people's homes and **helps** them there. Jason **isn't working** now. He's still **attending** college. He's in his last year. He's **studying** to be a lawyer. After classes every day, he **studies** at home or **goes** to the law library at his college. He's **going to graduate** next June. When he **graduates,** he **will have** to take a special exam for lawyers. If he **passes** it, he**'ll get** a good job and **make**

(continued)

good money. But when he **starts** to work, he**'ll have** to pay back student loans. For now, they**'re** both **living** on Katie's salary.

Katie and Jason **are saving** money little by little. They**'re planning** to buy a house in a suburb some day. They **are** also **thinking** about having two children in the future. But they want to be financially stable before they **have** children. Their parents sometimes **offer** to help them, but they **don't want** to depend on their parents. Because Jason is so busy with his studies and Katie is so busy with her job, they rarely **go** out. Staying at home **helps** them save money.

7.7 | Comparison of Tenses

Uses

Examples	Explanation
	Use the simple present tense:
a. Katie **works** as a nurse. Jason **studies** law. Lawyers **make** a lot of money in the U.S.	a. with facts
b. Grown children **don't like** to depend on their parents.	b. with customs
c. Jason **goes** to the library almost every day.	c. with habits and regular activities
d. Jason and Katie **have** a lot of responsibilities now.	d. with nonaction verbs
e. When Jason **graduates,** he will look for a job.	e. in a time clause or an *if* clause when talking about the future
	Use the present continuous tense:
a. I **am reviewing** verb tenses now.	a. with an action in progress now, at this moment
b. Jason and Katie **are saving** money to buy a house. They **are planning** to move to a suburb.	b. with a long-term action that is in progress; it may not be happening at this exact moment
	Use *will* for the future:
a. Katie thinks Jason **will be** a good lawyer.	a. with predictions
b. The law exam **will be** in March.	b. with facts
c. "I**'ll always** love you, Katie," says Jason.	c. with promises
d. "I**'ll help** you in the kitchen," says Katie.	d. with an offer to help
e. What will you do next year? I**'ll** cross that bridge when I get to it.	e. when you don't have a previous plan; when you decide what to do at the time of speaking
	Use *be going to* for the future:
a. I think they **are going to have** a wonderful life.	a. with predictions
b. For many years, they **are going to receive** bills for student loans.	b. with facts
c. Jason **is going to look** for a job next year.	c. with plans

Forms

Simple Present Tense	Present Continuous Tense
Jason **studies** law.	They **are saving** money to buy a house.
He **doesn't study** medicine.	They **aren't saving** to buy a new car.
Does he **study** every day?	**Are** they **saving** for a vacation?
Yes, he **does.**	No, they **aren't.**
Where **does** he **study?**	How **are** they **saving** money?
Why **doesn't** he **study** medicine?	Why **aren't** they **saving** to buy a car?
Who **studies** medicine?	Who **is saving** money?

Future with *Will*	Future with *Be Going To*
Jason **will graduate** next year.	They **are going to buy** a house.
He **won't graduate** this year.	They **aren't going to buy** a new car.
Will he **graduate** in January?	**Are** they **going to buy** a house in the city?
No, he **won't.**	No, they **aren't.**
When **will** he **graduate?**	Where **are** they **going to buy** a house?
Why **won't** he **graduate** in January?	Why **aren't** they **going to buy** a house in the city?
Who **will graduate** in January?	Who **is going to buy** a house?

EXERCISE 21 Fill in the blanks with the correct tense and form of the verb in parentheses ( ).

EXAMPLE Jason ___*is going to graduate*___ next year.
(graduate)

1. He _____ a good job when he _____.
   (have)   (graduate)

2. He _____ in the library.
   (often/study)

3. Jason and Katie _____ out.
   (rarely/go)

4. They _____ their money now.
   (save)

5. They _____ about buying a house.
   (think)

6. They _____ it's better to live in a suburb.
   (think)

EXERCISE 22   Fill in the blanks with the negative form of the underlined verb.

EXAMPLE   They <u>are</u> young. They _____*aren't*_____ old.

1. They <u>have</u> an apartment now. They _____ a house.

2. They <u>want</u> children, but they _____ children right now.

3. Katie <u>is working</u>. Jason _____ now. He's going to school.

4. They <u>depend</u> on each other. They _____ on their parents.

5. Jason <u>will graduate</u> in June. He _____ in January.

EXERCISE 23   Read each statement. Then write a *yes/no* question with the words in parentheses ( ). Write a short answer.

EXAMPLE   Katie <u>works</u> as a nurse. (in a hospital)
Does she work in a hospital? No, she doesn't. _____

1. Jason <u>is</u> a student. (Katie)

_____

2. Jason <u>is attending</u> college now. (Katie)

_____

3. Jason <u>will have</u> a job. (a good job)

_____

4. They <u>are thinking</u> about buying a house. (about having children)

_____

5. They <u>are going to have</u> children. (five children)

_____

EXERCISE **24**   Read each statement. Then write a *wh-* question about the words in parentheses ( ). An answer is not necessary.

EXAMPLE   Katie <u>works</u> as a nurse. (Where)
Where does she work as a nurse?

1. They <u>are saving</u> their money. (why)

2. They <u>don't want</u> to depend on their parents. (why)

3. Jason <u>will make</u> good money. (when)

4. Jason <u>wants</u> to be a lawyer. (why)

5. Katie <u>isn't going to work</u> when her children are small. (why)

6. Jason <u>will pay</u> back his student loans. (when)

7. They <u>don't go</u> out very much. (why)

8. Jason <u>is attending</u> college. (what college)

9. He <u>is going to graduate</u>. (when)

10. Jason <u>isn't earning</u> money now. (who)

11. Someone <u>wants</u> to help them. (who)

12. They <u>are learning</u> about responsibilities. (how)

1. Future patterns with *will*

AFFIRMATIVE:	He **will buy** a car.
NEGATIVE:	He **won't buy** a used car.
YES/NO QUESTION:	**Will** he **buy** a new car?
SHORT ANSWER:	Yes, he **will.**
WH- QUESTION:	When **will** he **buy** a car?
NEGATIVE QUESTION:	Why **won't** he **buy** a used car?
SUBJECT QUESTION:	Who **will buy** a car?

2. Future patterns with *be going to*

AFFIRMATIVE:	He **is going to buy** a car.
NEGATIVE:	He **isn't going to buy** a used car.
YES/NO QUESTION:	**Is** he **going to buy** a new car?
SHORT ANSWER:	Yes, he **is.**
WH- QUESTION:	When **is** he **going to buy** a car?
NEGATIVE QUESTION:	Why **isn't** he **going to buy** a used car?
SUBJECT QUESTION:	Who **is going to buy** a car?

3. Uses of *be going to* and *will*

Use	Will	Be Going To
Prediction	You **will become** rich and famous.	You **are going to become** rich and famous.
Fact	The sun **will set** at 6:32 p.m. tonight	The sun **is going to set** at 6:32 p.m. tonight.
Plan		I'm **going to buy** a new car next month.
Promise	I **will help** you tomorrow.	
Offer to help	A: I can't open the door. B: I'll **open** it for you.	
No previous plan	A: I need to go to the store. B: I'll **go** with you.	

4. Review the simple present tense and the present continuous tense on page 181.

1. Don't use *be* with a future verb.

   I will ~~be~~ go.

2. Use *be* in a future sentence that has no other verb.

He will _{be} angry.

There will _{be} a party soon.

3. Don't combine *will* and *be going to*.

He ~~will~~ ^{is} going to leave.   OR   *He will leave.*

4. Don't use the present tense for a future action.

I'm going home now. I ^{'ll} see you later.

5. Don't use the future tense after *when* or *if*.

When they ~~will~~ go home, they will watch TV.

6. Use a form of *be* with *going to*.

He _{is} going to help me.

7. Use *to* after *going*.

I'm going _{to} study on Saturday.

8. Use correct word order for questions.

Why ~~you aren't~~ ^{aren't you} going to eat lunch?

LESSON 7 TEST / REVIEW

PART 1   Find the mistakes with the underlined words and correct them. Not every sentence has a mistake. If the sentence is correct, write *C*.

EXAMPLES   I ~~will going to~~ ^{am} buy a newspaper.
If you're too tired to cook, <u>I'll do</u> it.   *C*

1. When <u>you will</u> write your composition?

2. We <u>will be buy</u> a new car soon.

3. Will you going to eat dinner tonight?

4. When he will leave, he will turn off the light.

5. I going to take a vacation soon.

6. Is he going to use the computer?

7. They're going graduate soon.

8. I will happy when I will know more English.

9. I'm going on vacation. I will going to leave next Friday.

10. I'll write you a letter when I arrive.

11. There will a test soon.

12. I'll help you tomorrow.

PART 2 Fill in the blanks with *will* or a form of *be + going to*. In some cases, both answers are possible.

EXAMPLES   I believe the next president _____*will* OR *is going to*_____ be a Democrat.

You can't move your piano alone. I _____*'ll*_____ help you do it.

1. We _____ eat in a new restaurant tomorrow. Do you want to go with us?

2. My friend is planning her wedding. She _____ invite 150 guests to her wedding.

3. I promise I _____ clean my room tomorrow.

4. If you come to work late every day, you _____ lose your job.

5. You don't know anything about computers? Come to my house.

   I _____ teach you.

6. The teacher _____ give a test next Friday.

7. Next week we _____ begin Lesson Eight.

8. Mother: Please call me when you arrive.

   Daughter: Don't worry, Mom. I _____ call you as soon as I arrive.

9. We're planning a picnic, but I think it _____ rain tomorrow.

PART 3 Fill in the blanks with the negative form of the underlined word.

  EXAMPLE She will get married in church. She _____won't get_____ married at home.

  1. She is going to invite all her relatives. She _____ all her friends.

  2. He will wear a tuxedo. He _____ a suit.

  3. I am going to buy a gift. I _____ dishes.

  4. I'll help you tomorrow. I _____ you today.

  5. You are going to meet my parents. You _____ my brothers.

PART 4 Read each statement. Then write a *yes/no* question about the words in parentheses ( ). Write a short answer.

  EXAMPLE She will write a letter. (a postcard) (no)
  Will she write a postcard? No, she won't.

  1. They will send a gift. (money) (no)

  _____

  2. You're going to invite your friends. (relatives) (yes)

  _____

  3. They are going to receive gifts. (open the gifts) (yes)

  _____

  4. They will need things for their kitchen. (for their bathroom) (yes)

  _____

  5. There will be a party after the wedding. (food at the party) (yes)

  _____

PART 5 Read each statement. Then write a question with the words in parentheses ( ). No answer is necessary.

  EXAMPLE I'm going to buy something. (What)
  What are you going to buy?

  1. They will use the money. (How)

  _____

2. I'm going to send a gift. (What kind of gift)

_____

3. They will thank us. (When)

_____

4. They're going to get married. (Where)

_____

5. They aren't going to open the gifts at the wedding. (Why)

_____

6. There will be a lot of people at the wedding. (How many people)

_____

7. Some people will give money. (Who)

_____

TEST ON COMPARISON OF TENSES

PART 1   Read the following letter. Fill in the blanks with the simple present, the present continuous, or the future tense.

Dear Judy,

Please excuse me for not writing sooner. I rarely _____*have*_____
                                                   (example: have)

time to sit and write a letter. My husband _____ on his
                                              (1 work)

car now, and the baby _____. So now I
                         (2 sleep)

_____ a few free moments.
   (3 have)

I _____ a student now. I _____
      (4 be)   *(5 go)*

to Kennedy College twice a week. The school _____ a
                                               (6 be)

few blocks from my house. I usually _____ to school,
                                       (7 walk)

but sometimes I _____ . My mother usually
                   (8 drive)

_____ the baby when I'm in school. This semester I
   (9 watch)

_____ English and math. Next semester I
   (10 study)

_____ a computer course. I _____
   (11 take)   *(12 think)*

knowledge about computers _____ me find a good job.
                             (13 help)

When the semester _____ over, we _____
(14 be)   (15 go)

to Canada for vacation. We _____ my husband's sister.
(16 visit)

She _____ in Montreal. We _____
(17 live)   (18 spend)

Christmas with her family this year. When we _____ to
(19 get)

Montreal, I _____ you a postcard.
(20 send)

Please write and tell me what is happening in your life.
Love,
Barbara

PART 2 Fill in the blanks with the negative form of the underlined verb.

EXAMPLE Barbara's a student. She _____ *isn't* _____ a teacher.

1. She's <u>writing</u> a letter now. She _____ a composition.

2. Her mother sometimes <u>takes</u> care of her baby. Her father _____
_____ care of her baby.

3. They're going to <u>visit</u> her husband's sister. They _____
_____ her mother.

4. She <u>goes</u> to Kennedy College. She _____ to Truman
College.

5. Barbara and her husband <u>live</u> in the U.S. They _____
in Canada.

6. Her family <u>will go</u> to Montreal. They _____ to
Toronto.

PART 3 Read each statement. Then write a *yes/no* question with the words
in parentheses ( ). Write a short answer, based on the letter.

EXAMPLE Barbara's studying English. (math)
Is she studying math? Yes, she is.

1. The baby's sleeping. (her husband)

_____

2. She sometimes drives to school. (ever/walk to school)

_____

3. She's going to take a computer course next semester. (a math class)

_____

4. She'll go to Canada. (Montreal)

_____

5. She's going to send Judy a postcard. (a letter)

_____

6. She sometimes writes letters. (write a letter/now)

_____

7. Her sister-in-law lives in Canada. (in Toronto)

_____

PART 4 Read each statement. Then write a *wh-* question with the words in parentheses ( ). Write an answer, based on the letter.

EXAMPLE   She goes to college. (Where)

A: *Where does she go to college?*

B: *She goes to Kennedy College.*

1. Her baby's sleeping. (What/her husband/do)

A: _____

B: _____

2. She's taking two courses this semester. (What courses)

A: _____

B: _____

3. Someone watches her baby. (Who)

A: _____

B: _____

4. She's going to take a course next semester. (What course)

A: _____

B: _____

5. They'll go on vacation for Christmas. (Where)

A: _____

B: _____

6. Her husband's sister lives in another city. (Where/she)

A: _____

B: _____

7. She doesn't usually drive to school. (Why)

A: _____

B: _____

EXPANSION ACTIVITIES

Classroom Activities

1. Check (✓) the activities that you plan to do soon. Find a partner. Ask your partner for information about the items he or she checked off. Report something interesting to the class about your partner's plans.

EXAMPLE ✓ move
When are you going to move?
Why are you going to move?
Are your friends going to help you?
Are you going to rent a truck?
Where are you going to move to?

a. _____ get married

b. _____ go back to my country

c. _____ spend a lot of money

d. _____ write a letter

e. _____ buy something (a computer, a DVD player, a TV, an answering machine, etc.)

f. _____ go to a party

g. _____ have a job interview

h. _____ transfer to another college

i. _____ become a citizen

j. _____ eat in a restaurant

2. Role-play the following characters. Practice the future tense.

   a. Fortune-teller and young woman. The woman wants to know her future.

   b. Man proposing marriage to a woman. The man is making promises.

   c. Teenager and parents. The teenager wants to go to a party on Saturday night.

   d. Politician and voter. The politician wants votes.

   e. Landlord and a person who wants to rent an apartment. The person wants to know what the landlord will do to fix up the apartment.

3. What are your concerns and plans for the future? Write one or two sentences (statements or questions) for each of the categories in the box below. Then find a partner. Discuss your concerns and plans with your partner.

Job/Career	*Where will I work if I lose my present job?*
Money	
Learning English	
Home	
Family and children	
Health	
Fun and recreation	
Other	

4. Imagine that you are going to buy a gift for someone in the following circumstances. What gift would you buy? Find a partner and compare your list of gifts to your partner's list.

   a. a friend in the hospital after surgery _____

   b. a couple with a new baby _____

   c. a nephew graduating from high school _____

   d. a friend getting married for the second time _____

   e. a friend moving into a new apartment _____

   f. a family that invites you to dinner at their house _____

Talk About it

1. In a small group or with the entire class, talk about gift-giving customs in your native culture. What kind of gifts do people give for weddings? How much money do they spend? Do newlyweds open presents at the wedding? Do they send thank-you cards? What kind of gifts do people give for other occasions?

2. Once a couple marries, both people often work. Sometimes only the man or only the woman works. In your native culture, does a woman ever support a man financially? Discuss.

Outside Activity

Use the third classroom activity above to interview an American about his or her concerns about the future. What is he or she worried about?

Internet Activities

Find a bridal or wedding registry on the Internet. What kind of gifts can a couple register for? What are the prices?

Additional Activities at **http://elt.thomson.com/gic**

Appendices

APPENDIX A

The Verb *GET*

Get has many meanings. Here is a list of the most common ones:
• get something = receive   I got a letter from my father.
• get + (to) place = arrive   I got home at six. What time do you get to school?
• get + object + infinitive = persuade   She got him to wash the dishes.

• get + past participle = become
    get acquainted   get worried   get hurt
    get engaged   get lost   get bored
    get married   get accustomed to   get confused
    get divorced   get used to   get scared
    get tired   get dressed
    They got married in 1989.

• get + adjective = become
    get hungry   get sleepy
    get rich   get dark
    get nervous   get angry
    get well   get old
    get upset   get fat
    It gets dark at 6:30.

• get an illness = catch   While she was traveling, she got malaria.

• get a joke or an idea = understand
    Everybody except Tom laughed at the joke. He didn't get it.
    The boss explained the project to us, but I didn't get it.

Continued

- get ahead = advance
    - He works very hard because he wants to get ahead in his job.

- get along (well) (with someone) = have a good relationship
    - She doesn't get along with her mother-in-law.
    - Do you and your roommate get along well?

- get around to something = find the time to do something
    - I wanted to write my brother a letter yesterday, but I didn't get around to it.

- get away = escape
    - The police chased the thief, but he got away.

- get away with something = escape punishment
    - He cheated on his taxes and got away with it.

- get back = return
    - He got back from his vacation last Saturday.

- get back at someone = get revenge
    - My brother wants to get back at me for stealing his girlfriend.

- get back to someone = communicate with someone at a later time
    - The boss can't talk to you today. Can she get back to you tomorrow?

- get by = have just enough but nothing more
    - On her salary, she's just getting by. She can't afford a car or a vacation.

- get in trouble = be caught and punished for doing something wrong
    - They got in trouble for cheating on the test.

- get in(to) = enter a car
    - She got in the car and drove away quickly.

- get out (of) = leave a car
    - When the taxi arrived at the theater, everyone got out.

- get on = seat yourself on a bicycle, motorcycle, horse
    - She got on the motorcycle and left.

- get on = enter a train, bus, airplane
    - She got on the bus and took a seat in the back.

- get off = leave a bicycle, motorcycle, horse, train, bus, airplane
    - They will get off the train at the next stop.

- get out of something = escape responsibility
    - My boss wants me to help him on Saturday, but I'm going to try to get out of it.

- get over something = recover from an illness or disappointment
    - She has the flu this weak. I hope she gets over it soon.

- get rid of someone or something = free oneself of someone or something undesirable
    - My apartment has roaches, and I can't get rid of them.

- get through (to someone) = communicate, often by telephone
    She tried to explain the harm of eating fast food to her son, but she couldn't get
        through to him.
    I tried to call my mother many times, but her line was busy. I couldn't get through.

- get through (with something) = finish
    I can meet you after I get through with my homework.

- get together = meet with another person
    I'd like to see you again. When can we get together?

- get up = arise from bed
    He woke up at 6 o'clock, but he didn't get up until 6:30.

APPENDIX B

MAKE and *DO*

Some expressions use *make.* Others use *do.*	
Make	**Do**
make a date/an appointment	do (the) homework
make a plan	do an exercise
make a decision	do the dishes
make a telephone call	do the cleaning, laundry, ironing, washing, etc.
make a reservation	do the shopping
make a meal (breakfast, lunch, dinner)	do one's best
make a mistake	do a favor
make an effort	do the right/wrong thing
make an improvement	do a job
make a promise	do business
make money	What do you do for a living? (asks about a job)
make noise	How do you do? (said when you
make the bed	meet someone for the first time)

Question Formation

1. Statements and Related Questions with a Main Verb.

Wh- Word	Do/Does/Did (n't)	Subject	Verb	Complement
When	does	She she	watches watch	TV. TV?
Where	do	My parents your parents	live live?	in Peru.
Who(m)	does	Your sister she	likes like?	someone.
Why	did	They they	left leave	early. early?
How many books	did	She she	found find?	some books.
What kind of car	did	He he	bought buy?	a car.
Why	didn't	She she	didn't go go	home. home?
Why	doesn't	He he	doesn't like like	tomatoes. tomatoes?

Subject	Verb (base form or -s form or past form)	Complement
Someone Who	has has	my book. my book?
Someone Who	needs needs	help. help?
Someone Who	took took	my pen. my pen?
One teacher Which teacher	speaks speaks	Spanish. Spanish?
Some men Which men	have have	a car. a car?
Some boys How many boys	saw saw	the movie. the movie?
Something What	happened. happened?	

2. Statements and Related Questions with the Verb *Be*.

Wh- Word	*Be*	Subject	*Be*	Complement
Where	is	She she?	is	in California.
Why	were	They they	were	hungry. hungry?
Why	isn't	He he	isn't	tired. tired?
When	was	He he	was	born in England. born?
		One student Who Which student	was was was	late. late? late?
		Some kids How many kids Which kids	were were were	afraid. afraid? afraid?

3. Statements and Related Questions with an Auxiliary (Aux) Verb and a Main Verb.

Wh- Word	Aux	Subject	Aux	Main Verb	Complement
Where	is	She she	is	running. running?	
When	will	They they	will	go go	on a vacation. on a vacation?
What	should	He he	should	do do?	something.
How many pills	can	You you	can	take take?	a pill.
Why	can't	You you	can't	drive drive	a car. a car?
		Someone Who	should should	answer answer	the question. the question?

Alphabetical List of Irregular Past Forms

Base Form	Past Form	Base Form	Past Form
arise	arose	forget	forgot
awake	awoke	forgive	forgave
be	was/were	freeze	froze
bear	bore	get	got
beat	beat	give	gave
become	became	go	went
begin	began	grind	ground
bend	bent	grow	grew
bet	bet	hang	hung[1]
bind	bound	have	had
bite	bit	hear	heard
bleed	bled	hide	hid
blow	blew	hit	hit
break	broke	hold	held
breed	bred	hurt	hurt
bring	brought	keep	kept
broadcast	broadcast	kneel	knelt (or kneeled)
build	built	know	knew
burst	burst	lay	laid
buy	bought	lead	led
cast	cast	leave	left
catch	caught	lend	lent
choose	chose	let	let
cling	clung	lie	lay
come	came	light	lit (or lighted)
cost	cost	lose	lost
creep	crept	make	made
cut	cut	mean	meant
deal	dealt	meet	met
dig	dug	mistake	mistook
do	did	pay	paid
draw	drew	put	put
drink	drank	quit	quit
drive	drove	read	read
eat	ate	ride	rode
fall	fell	ring	rang
feed	fed	rise	rose
feel	felt	run	ran
fight	fought	say	said
find	found	see	saw
fit	fit	seek	sought
flee	fled	sell	sold
fly	flew	send	sent

[1]*Hanged* is used as the past form to refer to punishment by death. *Hung* is used in other situations. She *hung* the picture on the wall.

Base Form	Past Form	Base Form	Past Form
forbid	forbade	set	set
shake	shook	stink	stank
shed	shed	strike	struck
shine	shone (or shined)	strive	strove
shoot	shot	swear	swore
shrink	shrank	sweep	swept
shut	shut	swim	swam
sing	sang	swing	swung
sink	sank	take	took
sit	sat	teach	taught
sleep	slept	tear	tore
slide	slid	tell	told
slit	slit	think	thought
speak	spoke	throw	threw
speed	sped	understand	understood
spend	spent	upset	upset
spin	spun	wake	woke
spit	spit	wear	wore
split	split	weave	wove
spread	spread	weep	wept
spring	sprang	win	won
stand	stood	wind	wound
steal	stole	withdraw	withdrew
stick	stuck	wring	wrung
sting	stung	write	wrote

APPENDIX E

Meanings of Modals and Related Words

- Ability, Possibility

   Can you drive a truck?

   You **can** get a ticket for speeding.

- Necessity, Obligation

   A driver **must** have a license (legal obligation)

   I **have** *to* buy a new car. (personal obligation)

- Permission

   You **can** park at a meter.

   You **can't** park at a bus stop.

- Possibility

   I **may** buy a new car soon.

   I **might** buy a Japanese car.

- Advice

   You **should** buy a new car. Your old car is in terrible condition.

- Permission Request

  May I borrow your car?

  Can I have the keys, please?

  Could I have the keys, please?

- Polite Request

  Would you teach me to drive?

  Could you show me your new car?

- Want

  What **would** you *like* to eat?

  I'd like a turkey sandwich.

Capitalization Rules

- The first word in a sentence: **My** friends are helpful.

- The word "I": My sister and **I** took a trip together.

- Names of people: **J**ulia **R**oberts; **G**eorge **W**ashington

- Titles preceding names of people: **D**octor (**D**r.) **S**mith; **P**resident **L**incoln; **Q**ueen **E**lizabeth; **M**r. **R**ogers; **M**rs. **C**arter

- Geographic names: the **U**nited **S**tates; **L**ake **S**uperior; **C**alifornia; the **R**ocky **M**ountains; the **M**ississippi **R**iver

  NOTE: The word "the" in a geographic name is not capitalized.

- Street names: **P**ennsylvania **A**venue (**A**ve.); **W**all **S**treet (**S**t.); **A**bbey **R**oad (**R**d.)

- Names of organizations, companies, colleges, buildings, stores, hotels: the **R**epublican **P**arty; **H**einle **T**homson; **D**artmouth **C**ollege; the **U**niversity of **W**isconsin; the **W**hite **H**ouse; **B**loomingdale's; the **H**ilton **H**otel

- Nationalities and ethnic groups: **M**exicans; **C**anadians; **S**paniards; **A**mericans; **J**ews; **K**urds; **E**skimos

- Languages: **E**nglish; **S**panish; **P**olish; **V**ietnamese; **R**ussian

- Months: **J**anuary; **F**ebruary

- Days: **S**unday; **M**onday

- Holidays: **C**hristmas; **I**ndependence **D**ay

- Important words in a title: **G**rammar in **C**ontext; **T**he **O**ld **M**an and the **S**ea; **R**omeo and **J**uliet; **T**he **S**ound of **M**usic

  NOTE: Capitalize "the" as the first word of a title.

Metric Conversion Chart

Length

When You Know	Symbol	Multiply by	To Find	Symbol
inches	in	2.54	centimeters	cm
feet	ft	30.5	centimeters	cm
feet	ft	0.3	meters	m
yards	yd	0.91	meters	m
miles	mi	1.6	kilometers	km
Metric:				
centimeters	cm	0.39	inches	in
centimeters	cm	0.03	feet	ft
meter	m	3.28	feet	ft
meters	m	1.09	yards	yd
kilometers	km	0.62	miles	mi

Note:
1 foot = 12 inches
1 yard = 3 feet or 36 inches

Area

When You Know	Symbol	Multiply by	To Find	Symbol
square inches	in^2	6.5	square centimeters	cm^2
square feet	ft^2	0.09	square meters	m^2
square yards	yd^2	0.8	square meters	m^2
square miles	mi^2	2.6	square kilometers	km^2
Metric:				
square centimeters	cm^2	0.16	square inches	in^2
square meters	m^2	10.76	square feet	ft^2
square meters	m^2	1.2	square yards	yd^2
square kilometers	km^2	0.39	square miles	mi^2

Continued

Weight (Mass)

When You Know	Symbol	Multiply by	To Find	Symbol
ounces	oz	28.35	grams	g
pounds	lb	0.45	kilograms	kg
Metric:				
grams	g	0.04	ounces	oz
kilograms	kg	2.2	pounds	lb
Note: 16 ounces = 1 pound				

Volume

When You Know	Symbol	Multiply by	To Find	Symbol
fluid ounces	fl oz	30.0	milliliters	mL
pints	pt	0.47	liters	L
quarts	qt	0.95	liters	L
gallons	gal	3.8	liters	L
Metric:				
milliliters	mL	0.03	fluid ounces	fl oz
liters	L	2.11	pints	pt
liters	L	1.05	quarts	qt
liters	L	0.26	gallons	gal

Temperature

When You Know	Symbol	Do this	To Find	Symbol
degrees Fahrenheit	°F	Subtract 32, then multiply by $5/9$	degrees Celsius	°C
Metric:				
degrees Celsius	°C	Multiply by $9/5$, then add 32	degrees Fahrenheit	°F

Sample temperatures	
Fahrenheit	**Celsius**
0	– 18
10	– 12
20	– 7
30	– 1
40	4
50	10
60	16
70	21
80	27
90	32
100	38

APPENDIX H

Prepositions of Time

- **in** the morning: He takes a shower *in* the morning.

- **in** the afternoon: He takes a shower *in* the afternoon.

- **in** the evening: He takes a shower *in* the evening.

- **at** night: He takes a shower *at* night.

- **in** the summer, fall, winter, spring: He takes classes *in* the summer.

- **on** that/this day: October 10 is my birthday. I became a citizen *on* that day.

- **on** the weekend: He studies *on* the weekend.

- **on** a specific day: His birthday is *on* March 5.

- **in** a month: His birthday is *in* March.

- **in** a year: He was born *in* 1978.

- **in** a century: People didn't use cars *in* the 19th century.

- **on** a day: I don't have class *on* Monday.

- **at** a specific time: My class begins *at* 12:30.

- **from** a time **to** another time: My class is *from* 12:30 *to* 3:30.

- **in** a number of hours, days, weeks, months, years: She will graduate *in* three weeks. (This means "after" three weeks.)

- **for** a number of hours, days, weeks, months, years: She was in Mexico *for* three weeks. (This means during the period of three weeks.)

- **by** a time: Please finish your test *by* 6 o'clock. (This means "no later than" 6 o'clock.)

- **until** a time: I lived with my parents *until* I came to the U.S. (This means "all the time before.")

- **during** the movie, class, meeting: He slept *during* the meeting.

- **about/around** 6 o'clock: The movie will begin *about* 6 o'clock. People will arrive *around* 5:45.

- **in** the past/future: *In* the past, she never exercised.

- **at** present: *At* present, the days are getting longer.

- **in** the beginning/end: *In* the beginning, she didn't understand the teacher at all.

- **at** the beginning/end of something: The semester beings *at* the beginning of September. My birthday is *at* the end of June.

- **before/after** a time: You should finish the job *before* Friday. The library will be closed *after* 6:00.

- **before/after** an action takes place: Turn off the lights *before* you leave. Wash the dishes *after* you finish dinner.

APPENDIX I

Glossary of Grammatical Terms

- **Adjective** An adjective gives a description of a noun.

   It's a *tall* tree.   He's an *old* man.   My neighbors are *nice*.

- **Adverb** An adverb describes the action of a sentence or an adjective or another adverb.

   She speaks English *fluently*.   I drive *carefully*.

   She speaks English *extremely* well.   She is *very* intelligent.

- **Adverb of Frequency** An adverb of frequency tells how often the action happens.

   I *never* drink coffee.   They *usually* take the bus.

- **Affirmative** means *yes*.

- **Apostrophe** ' We use the apostrophe for possession and contractions.

   My *sister's* friend is beautiful.   Today *isn't* Sunday.

- **Article** The definite article is *the*. The indefinite articles are *a* and *an*.

   I have *a* cat.   I ate *an* apple.   *The* president was in
   New York last weekend.

- **Auxiliary Verb** Some verbs have two parts: an auxiliary verb and a main verb.

  He *can't* study.   We *will* return.

- **Base Form** The base form, sometimes called the "simple" form, of the verb has no tense. It has no ending (-*s* or -*ed*): *be, go, eat, take, write.*

  I didn't *go* out.   He doesn't *know* the answer.

  You shouldn't *talk* loudly.

- **Capital Letter** A B C D E F G . . .

- **Clause** A clause is a group of words that has a subject and a verb. Some sentences have only one clause.

  She speaks Spanish.

  Some sentences have **a main clause** and a **dependent clause.**

MAIN CLAUSE	DEPENDENT CLAUSE (**reason clause**)
She found a good job	because she has computer skills.
MAIN CLAUSE	DEPENDENT CLAUSE (**time clause**)
She'll turn off the light	before she goes to bed.
MAIN CLAUSE	DEPENDENT CLAUSE (*if* **clause**)
I'll take you to the doctor	if you don't have your car on Saturday.

- **Colon** :

- **Comma** ,

- **Comparative Form** A comparative form of an adjective or adverb is used to compare two things.

  My house is *bigger* than your house.

  Her husband drives *faster* than she does.

- **Complement** The complement of the sentence is the information after the verb. It completes the verb phrase.

  He works *hard.*   I slept *for five hours.*   They are *late.*

- **Consonant** The following letters are consonants: *b, c, d, f, g, h, j, k, l, m, n, p, q, r, s, t, v, w, x, y, z.*

  NOTE: *y* is sometimes considered a vowel, as in the world *syllable.*

- **Contraction** A contraction is made up of two words put together with an apostrophe.

  He's my brother.   *You're* late.   They *won't* talk to me.

  (*He's = he is*)   (*You're = you are*)   (*won't = will not*)

- **Count Noun** Count nouns are nouns that we can count. They have a singular and a plural form.

  1 pen — 3 pens   1 table — 4 tables

- **Dependent Clause** See **Clause.**

- **Direct Object** A direct object is a noun (phrase) or pronoun that receives the action of the verb.

  We saw *the movie*.   You have *a nice car*.   I love *you*.

- **Exclamation Mark !**

- **Frequency words** Frequency words are *always, usually, often, sometimes, rarely, seldom, never*.

  I *never* drink coffee.   We *always* do our homework.

- **Hyphen –**

- **Imperative** An imperative sentence gives a command or instructions. An imperative sentence omits the word *you*.

  Come here.   *Don't be* late.   Please *sit* down.

- **Infinitive** An infinitive is *to* + base form.

  I want *to leave*.   You need *to be* here on time.

- **Linking Verb** A linking verb is a verb that links the subject to the noun or adjective after it. Linking verbs include *be, seem, feel, smell, sound, look, appear, taste*.

  She *is* a doctor.   She *seems* very intelligent.   She *looks* tired.

- **Modal** The modal verbs are *can, could, shall, should, will, would, may, might, must*.

  They *should* leave.   I *must* go.

- **Negative** means no.

- **Nonaction Verb** A nonaction verb has no action. We do not use a continuous tense (*be* + verb *-ing*) with a nonaction verb. The nonaction verbs are: *believe, cost, care, have, hear, know, like, love, matter, mean, need, own, prefer, remember, see, seem, think, understand, want*.

  She *has* a laptop.   We *love* our mother.

- **Noncount Noun** A noncount noun is a noun that we don't count. It has no plural form.

  She drank some *water*.   He prepared some *rice*.

  Do you need any *money*?

- **Noun** A noun is a person (*brother*), a place (*kitchen*) or a thing (*table*). Nouns can be either count (*1 table, 2 tables*) or noncount (*money, water*).

  My *brother* lives in California.   My *sisters* live in New York.

  I get *mail* from them.

- **Noun Modifier** A noun modifier makes a noun more specific.

  fire department   *Independence* Day   *can* opener

- **Noun Phrase** A noun phrase is a group of words that form the subject or object of the sentence.

  A very nice woman helped me at registration.

  I bought *a big box of candy*.

- **Object** The object of the sentence follows the verb. It receives the action of the verb.

  He bought *a car*.　　I saw *a movie*.　　I met *your brother*.

- **Object Pronoun** Use object pronouns (*me, you, him, her, it, us, them*) after the verb or preposition.

  He likes *her*.　　I saw the movie. Let's talk about *it*.

- **Parentheses ( )**

- **Paragraph** A paragraph is a group of sentences about one topic.

- **Participle, Present** The present participle is verb + *-ing*.

  She is *sleeping*.　　They were *laughing*.

- **Period .**

- **Phrase** A group of words that go together.

  Last month my sister came to visit.

  There is a strange car *in front of my house*.

- **Plural** Plural means more than one. A plural noun usually ends with *-s*.

  She has beautiful *eyes*.

- **Possessive Form** Possessive forms show ownership or relationship.

  Mary's coat is in the closet.　　*My* brother lives in Miami.

- **Preposition** A preposition is a short connecting word: *about, above, across, after, around, as, at, away, back, before, behind, below, by, down, for, from, in, into, like, of, off, on, out, over, to, under, up with*.

  The book is *on* the table.

- **Pronoun** A pronoun takes the place of a noun.

  I have a new car. I bought *it* last week.

  John likes Mary, but *she* doesn't like *him*.

- **Punctuation** Period . Comma , Colon : Semicolon ; Question Mark ? Exclamation Mark !

- **Question Mark ?**

- **Quotation Marks " "**

- **Regular Verb** A regular verb forms its past tense with *-ed*.

  He *worked* yesterday.　　I *laughed* at the joke.

- **s Form** A present-tense verb that ends in *-s* or *-es*.

  He *lives* in New York.　　She *watches* TV a lot.

- **Sense-Perception Verb** A sense-perception verb has no action. It describes a sense.

  She *feels* fine.　　The coffee *smells* fresh.　　The milk *tastes* sour.

- **Sentence** A sentence is a group of words that contains a subject[1] and a verb (at least) and gives a complete thought.

  SENTENCE: She came home.

  NOT A SENTENCE: When she came home

- **Simple Form of Verb** The simple form of the verb, also called the base form, has no tense; it never has an *-s*, *-ed*, or *-ing* ending.

  Did you *see* the movie?   I couldn't *find* your phone number.

- **Singular** Singular means one.

  She ate a *sandwich.*   I have one *television.*

- **Subject** The subject of the sentence tells who or what the sentence is about.

  My sister got married last April. *The wedding* was beautiful.

- **Subject Pronouns** Use subject pronouns (*I, you, he, she, it, we, you, they*) before a verb.

  They speak Japanese.   *We* speak Spanish.

- **Superlative Form** A superlative form of an adjective or adverb shows the number one item in a group of three or more.

  January is the *coldest* month of the year.

  My brother speaks English the *best* in my family.

- **Syllable** A syllable is a part of a word that has only one vowel sound. (Some words have only one syllable.)

  change (one syllable)   after (af·ter = 2 syllables)

  look (one syllable)   responsible (re·spon·si·ble = 4 syllables)

- **Tag Question** A tag question is a short question at the end of a sentence. It is used in conversation.

  You speak Spanish, *don't you?*   He's not happy, *is he?*

- **Tense** A verb has tense. Tense shows when the action of the sentence happened.

  SIMPLE PRESENT: She usually *works* hard.

  FUTURE: She *will work* tomorrow.

  PRESENT CONTINUOUS: She *is working* now.

  SIMPLE PAST: She *worked* yesterday.

- **Verb** A verb is the action of the sentence.

  He *runs* fast.   I *speak* English.

  Some verbs have no action. They are linking verbs. They connect the subject to the rest of the sentence.

  He *is* tall.   She *looks* beautiful.   You *seem* tired.

- **Vowel** The following letters are vowels: *a, e, i, o, u. Y* is sometimes considered a vowel (for example, in the word *syllable*).

---

[1] In an imperative sentence, the subject *you* is omitted: *Sit down. Come here.*

Verbs and Adjectives Followed by a Preposition

(be) accustomed to
(be) afraid of
agree with
(be) angry about
(be) angry at/with
approve of
argue about
(be) ashamed of
(be) aware of
believe in
(be) bored with/by
(be) capable of
care about/for
(be) compared to
complain about
(be) concerned about
concentrate on
consist of
count on
deal with
decide on
depend on/upon
dream about/of
(be) engaged to
(be) excited about
(be) familiar with
(be) famous for
feel like
(be) fond of
forget about

forgive someone for
(be) glad about
(be) good at
(be) happy about
hear about
hear of
hope for
(be) incapable of
insist on/upon
(be) interested in
(be) involved in
(be) jealous of
(be) known for
(be) lazy about
listen to
look at
look for
look forward to
(be) mad about
(be) mad at
(be) made from/of
(be) married to
object to
participate in
plan on
pray to
pray for
(be) prepared for
prohibit from
protect someone from

(be) proud of
recover from
(be) related to
rely on/upon
(be) responsible for
(be) sad about
(be) satisfied with
(be) scared of
(be) sick of
(be) sorry about
(be) sorry for
speak about
speak to/with
succeed in
(be) sure of/about
(be) surprised at
take care of
talk about
talk to/with
thank someone for
(be) thankful to someone for
think about/of
(be) tired of
(be) upset about
(be) upset with
(be) used to
wait for
warn about
(be) worried about
worry about

The United States of America: Major Cities

AL	Alabama	IN	Indiana	NE	Nebraska	SC	South Carolina
AK	Alaska	IA	Iowa	NV	Nevada	SD	South Dakota
AZ	Arizona	KS	Kansas	NH	New Hampshire	TN	Tennessee
AR	Arkansas	KY	Kentucky	NJ	New Jersey	TX	Texas
CA	California	LA	Louisiana	NM	New Mexico	UT	Utah
CO	Colorado	ME	Maine	NY	New York	VT	Vermont
CT	Connecticut	MD	Maryland	NC	North Carolina	VA	Virginia
DE	Delaware	MA	Massachusetts	ND	North Dakota	WA	Washington
FL	Florida	MI	Michigan	OH	Ohio	WV	West Virginia
GA	Georgia	MN	Minnesota	OK	Oklahoma	WI	Wisconsin
HI	Hawaii	MS	Mississippi	OR	Oregon	WY	Wyoming
ID	Idaho	MO	Missouri	PA	Pennsylvania	DC*	District of
IL	Illinois	MT	Montana	RI	Rhode Island		Columbia

*The District of Columbia is not a state. Washington D.C. is the capital of the United States.
Note: Washington D.C. and Washigton state are not the same.

Index

Photo Credits

1: Paul Barton/Corbis; *2*: Courtesy Sandra Elbaum; *5*, Esbin-Anderson/The Image Works; *7*, James Marshall/The Image Works; *8*, Photodisc/Getty Images; *11*, Spencer Grant/PhotoEdit, Inc.; *16*, Heinle Thomson/Image Bank; *19*, David Young Wolff/Photo Edit, Inc.; *25*, Bob Daemmrich/The Image Works; *28*, Susan Van Etten/PhotoEdit, Inc.; *41*, Galen Rowell/CORBIS; *42*, *left*, TAXI/Getty Images, *middle*, Royalty Free/CORBIS, *right*, Phillip James Corwin/CORBIS; *43*, Mannie Garcia/Reuters/CORBIS; *48*, Heinle Thomson/Image Bank; *49*, Park Street/ PhotoEdit, Inc.; *52*, Getty Images; *57*, Royalty Free/CORBIS; *77*, © Dex Images, Inc./CORBIS; *78*, TAXI/Getty Images; *79*, Rudi Von Briel/PhotoEdit, Inc.; *81*, Jeff Greenberg/PhotoEdit, Inc.; *83*, Paul Barton/CORBIS; *85*, Sondra Dawes/The Image Works; *91*, Tom Carter/PhotoEdit, Inc.; *97*, Shelly Gazin/The Image Works; *101*, *top left*, Conrad Zobel/CORBIS, *bottom left*, Jeff Greenberg/PhotoEdit, Inc., *right*, Royalty Free/CORBIS; *102*, Bob Daemmrich/The Image Works; *103*, Royalty Free/CORBIS; *107*, Jeff Greenberg/The Image Works; *109*, Jeff Greenberg/PhotoEdit, Inc.; *113*, Richard Hutchings/PhotoEdit, Inc.; *119*, Dwayne Newton/PhotoEdit, Inc.; *122*, Frank Siteman/PhotoEdit, Inc.; *131*, Ariel Skelley/CORBIS; *132*, Royalty Free/CORBIS; *134*, Michael Newman/PhotoEdit, Inc.; *137*, *left*, Tony Freeman/PhotoEdit, Inc., *right*, Michael Newman/PhotoEdit, Inc.; *139*, Ariel Skelley/CORBIS; *142*, Marty Hatner/The Image Works; *143*, Jeff Greenberg/PhotoEdit, Inc.; *145*, Reed Kaestner/CORBIS; *147*, David Young Wolff/PhotoEdit, Inc.; *153*, Bonnie Kaman/PhotoEdit, Inc.; *156*, Mark Reinstein/The Image Works; *159*, *top/bottom*, TAXI/Getty Images; *160*, David Young Wolff/PhotoEdit, Inc.; *178*, Michael Keller/CORBIS; *179*, TAXI/Getty Images; *189*, Royalty Free/CORBIS; *190*, Eric Larrayadiell/STONE/Getty Images; *194*, Bob Daemmrich/The Image Works; *195*, Jeff Greenberg/The Image Works; *196*, Heinle Thomson/Image Bank; *197*, James Pickerell/The Image Works; *198*, Nancy Richmond/The Image Works; *199*, Frank Siteman/PhotoEdit, Inc.; *201*, Stockbyte/Superstock; *208*, Dave Bartruff/CORBIS; *209*, Courtesy Sandra Elbaum; *212*, Robert Brenner/PhotoEdit, Inc.; *223*, Bettmann/CORBIS; *224*, Underwood and Underwood/CORBIS; *229*, *left*, CORBIS, *right*, Bettmann/CORBIS; *233*, Hulton Archives/Getty Images; *236*, James P. Blair/CORBIS; *237*, *left*, Bettmann/CORBIS, *right*, CORBIS; *238*, AFP Getty Images; *241*, Alex Wong/Getty Images; *248*, Time Life Pictures/Getty Images; *251*, STONE/Getty Images; *252*, Bob Daemmrich/The Image Works; *263*, Iannen Maury/The Image Works; *264*, Gary D. Landsman/CORBIS; *267*, John Schults/Reuters/Corbis; *272*, Spencer Grant/PhotoEdit, Inc.; *283*, Dennis MacDonald/PhotoEdit, Inc.; *284*, Chuck Savage/CORBIS; *288*, Rhoda Sidney/The Image Works; *293*, Mark Antman/The Image Works; *296*, Bonn Sequenz/Imapress/The Image Works; *303*, Johnny Crawford/The Image Works; *307*, Rob Levine/CORBIS; *308*, Comstock/Getty Images; *310*, *chart*, © Hemera Photos; *318*, Michael Newman/PhotoEdit, Inc.; *320*, Stone/Getty Images; *325*, Robert Brenner/PhotoEdit, Inc.; *333*, Bettmann/CORBIS; *334*, Bettmann/CORBIS; *335*, Bettmann/CORBIS; *339*, Robert Holmes/CORBIS; *343*, Bettman; *345*, Geoffrey Clements/CORBIS; *348*, David Frazier/The Image Works; *355*, *top left*, Roger Bessmeyer/CORBIS, *bottom left*, Jim Zuckerman/CORBIS, *right*, Digitalvision/Getty Images; *357*, David Muench/CORBIS; *363*, *left*, STONE/Getty Images, *right*, Alan Schien Photography/CORBIS; *365*, Karen Huntt/CORBIS; *369*, Royalty Free/CORBIS; *370*, Cathy Melloan Resources/PhotoEdit, Inc.; *377*, Rolf Brueder/CORBIS; *378*, STONE/Getty Images; *379*, Michael Keller/CORBIS; *384*, Jeff Greenberg/PhotoEdit, Inc.; *387*, Heinle/Thomson Image Bank; *401*, Photodisc/Getty Images; *402*, Royalty Free/CORBIS